ISBN-10: 0-9971660-0-2

ISBN-13: 978-0-9971660-0-2

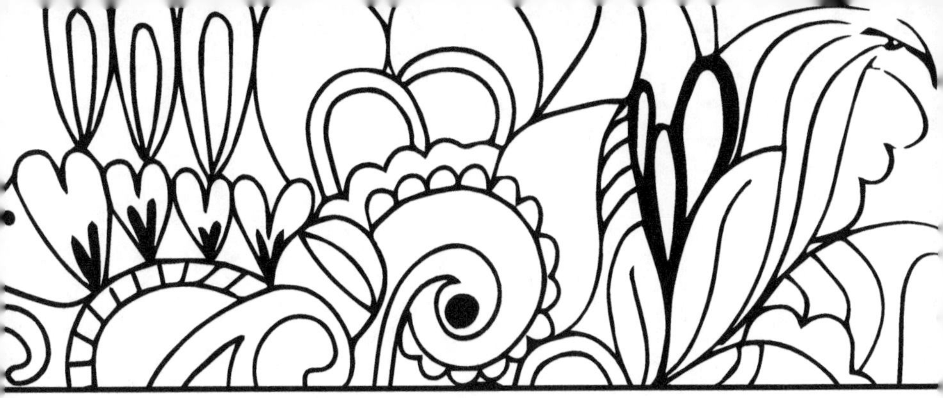

Calm Yourself:

COLORING FOR WHEN ADULTING SUCKS

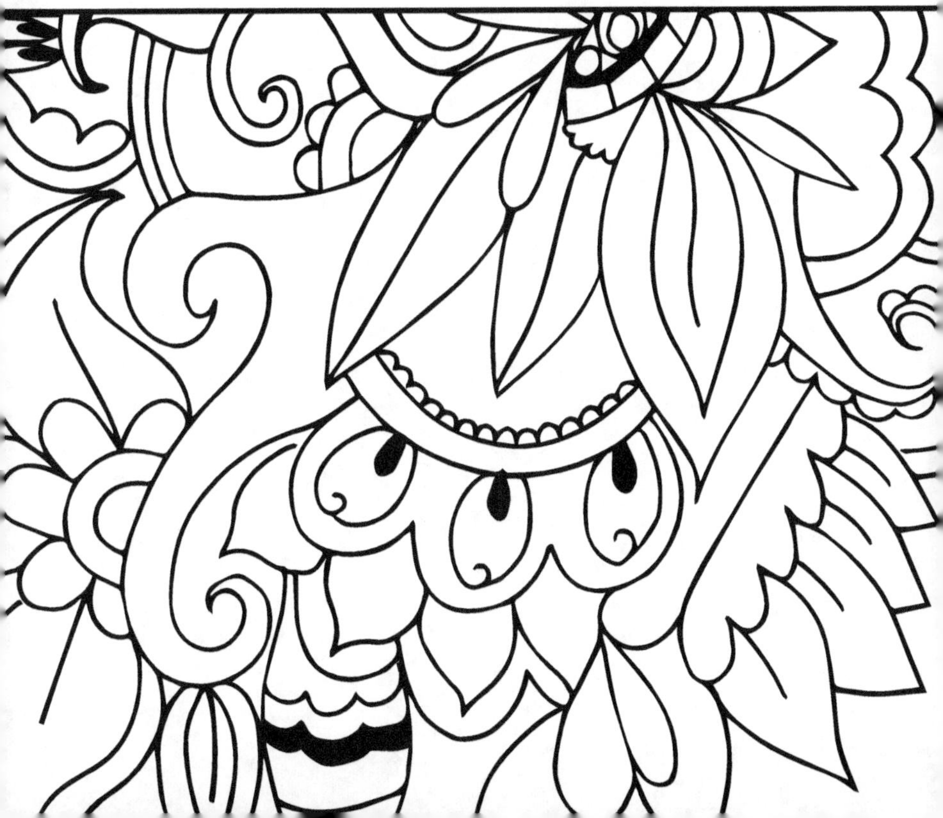

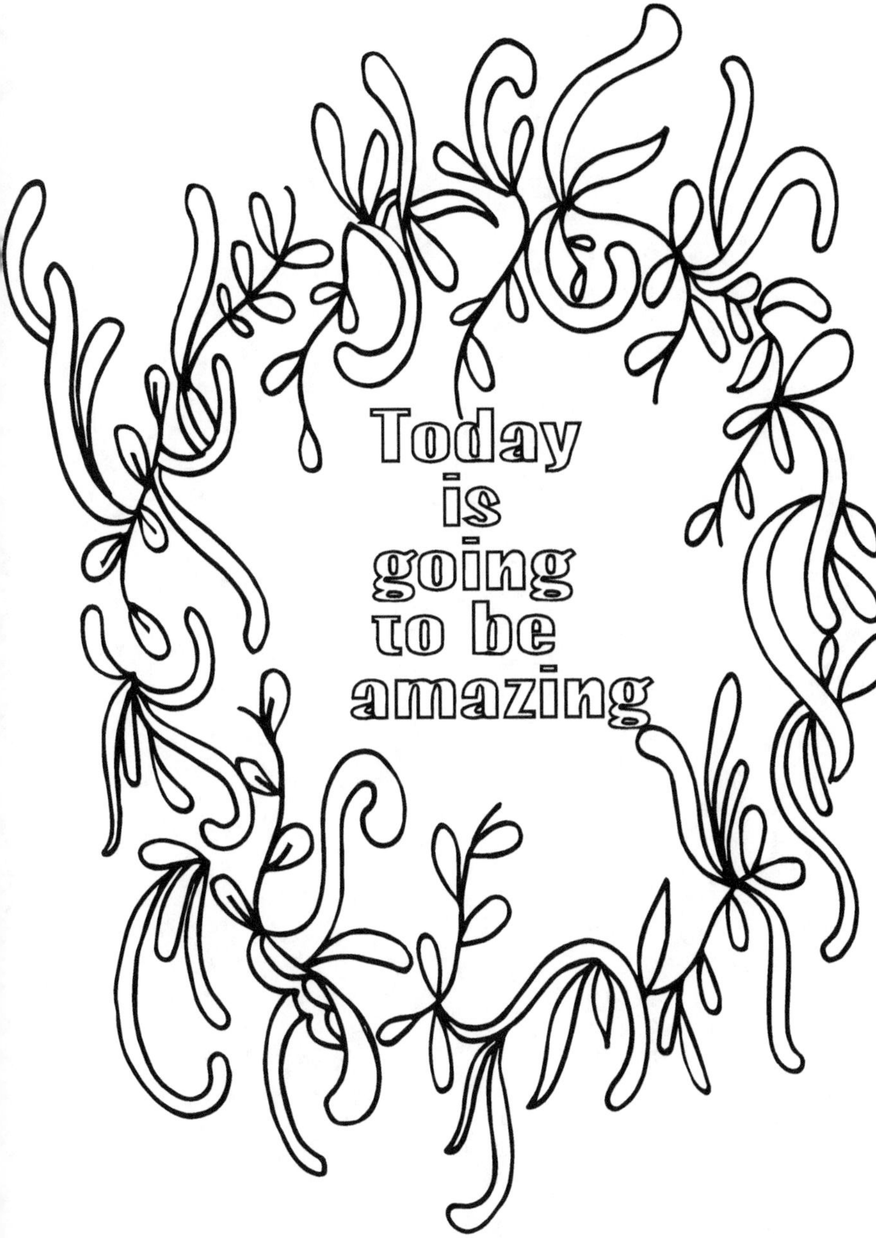
Today
is
going
to be
amazing

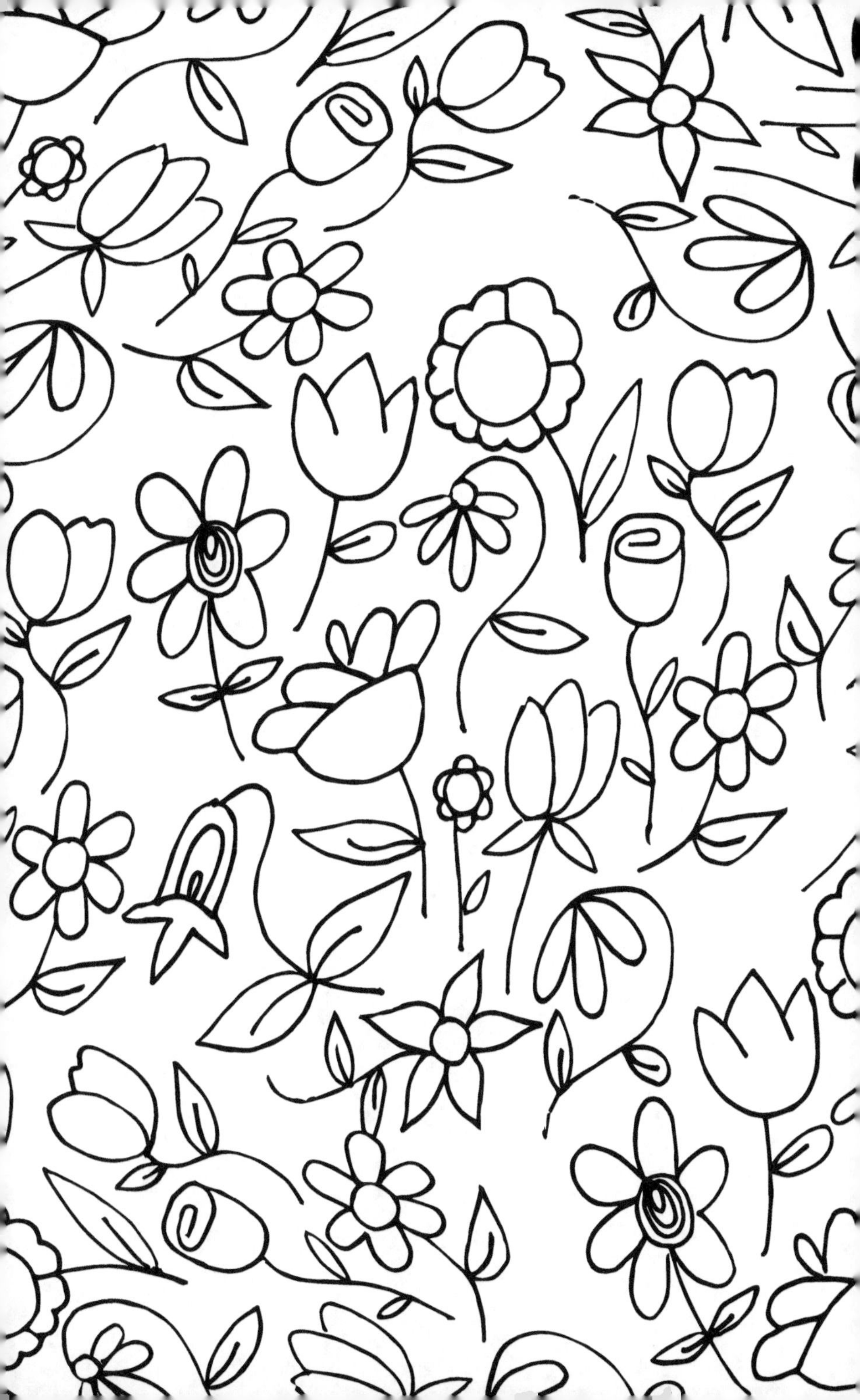

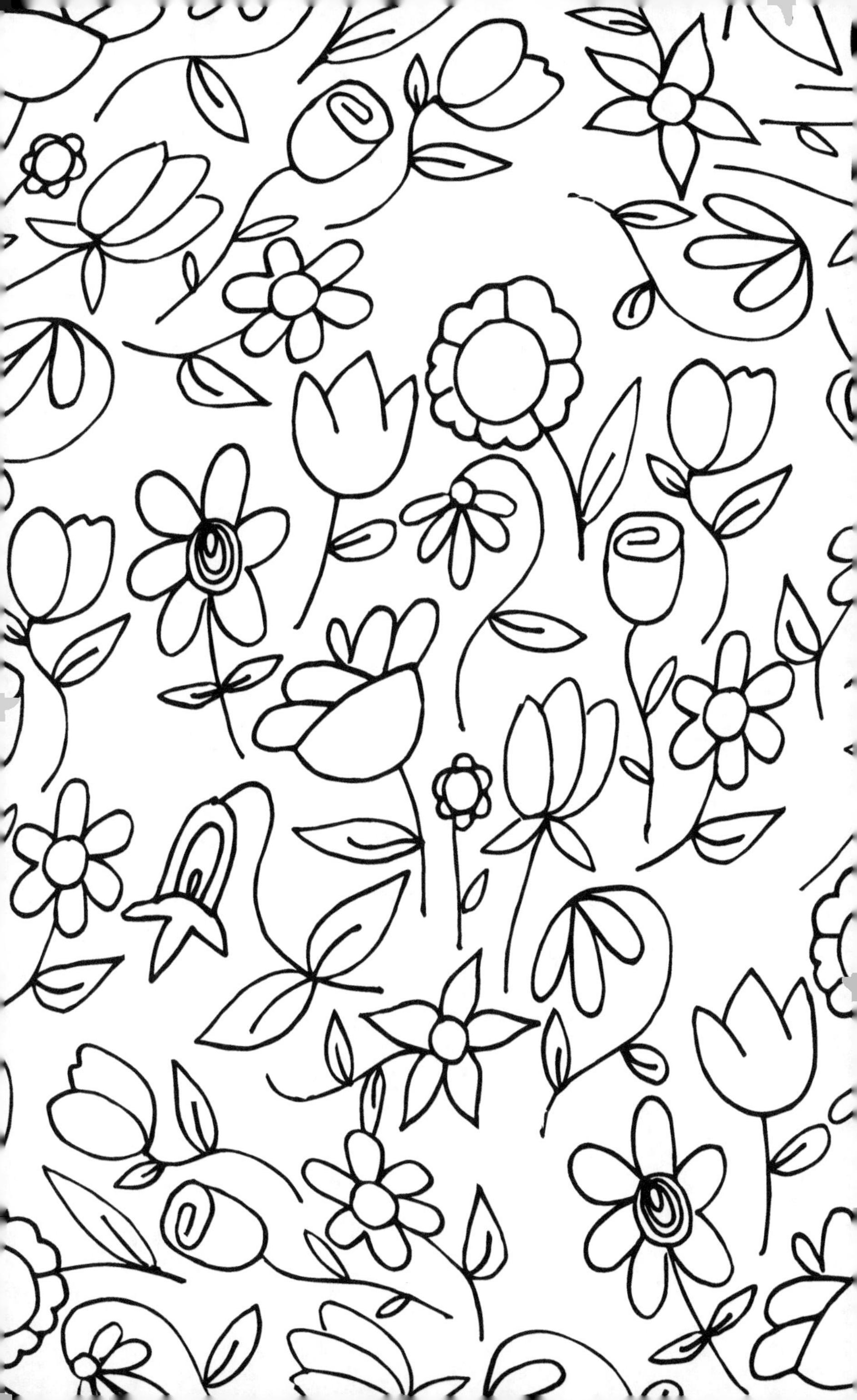

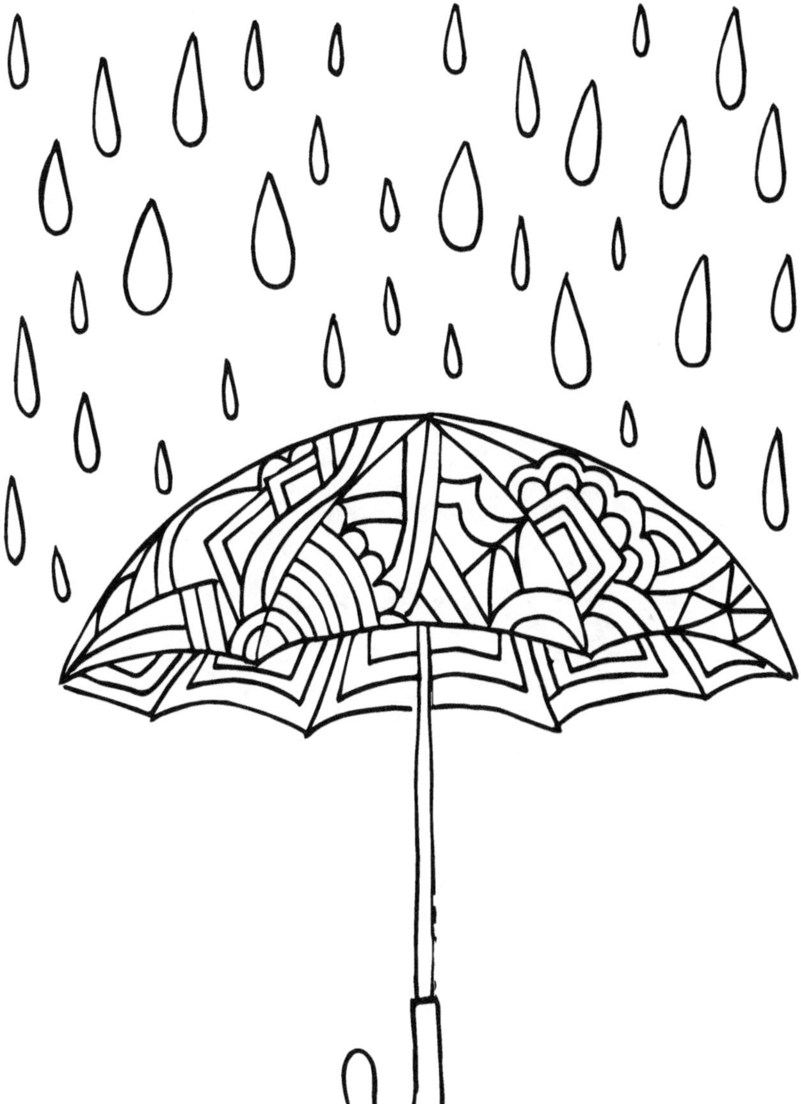

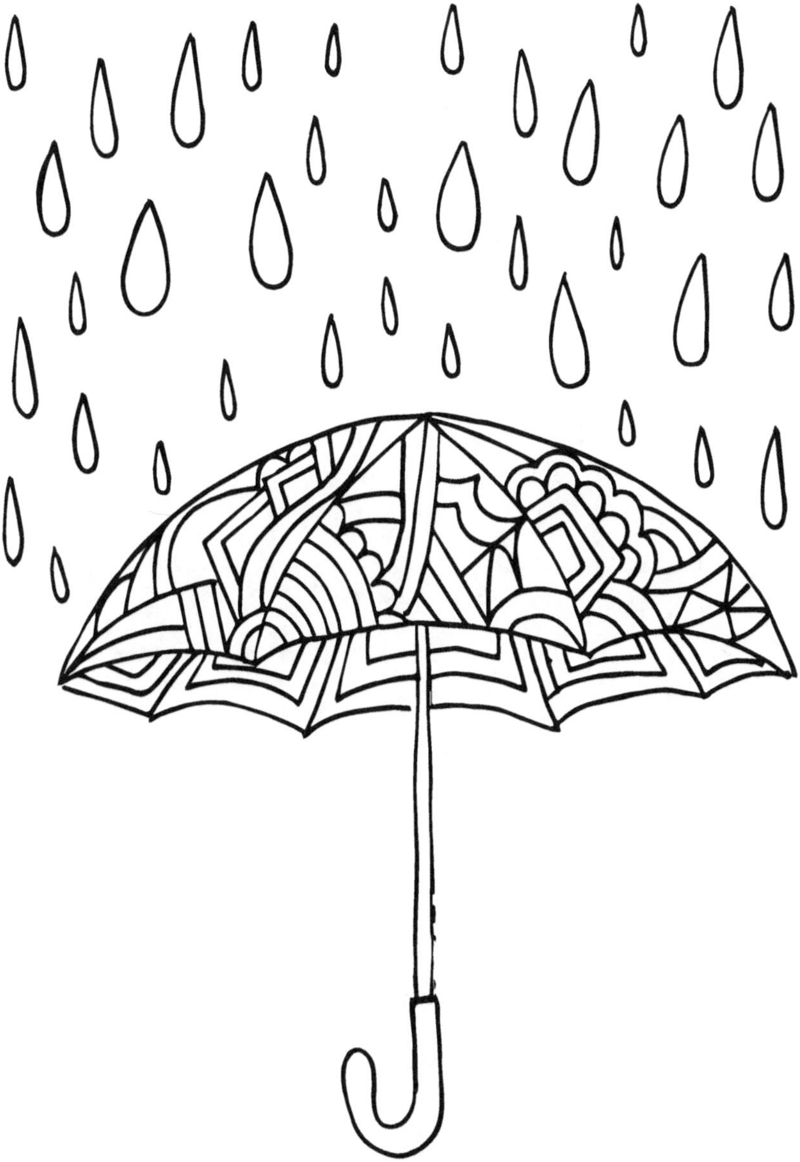

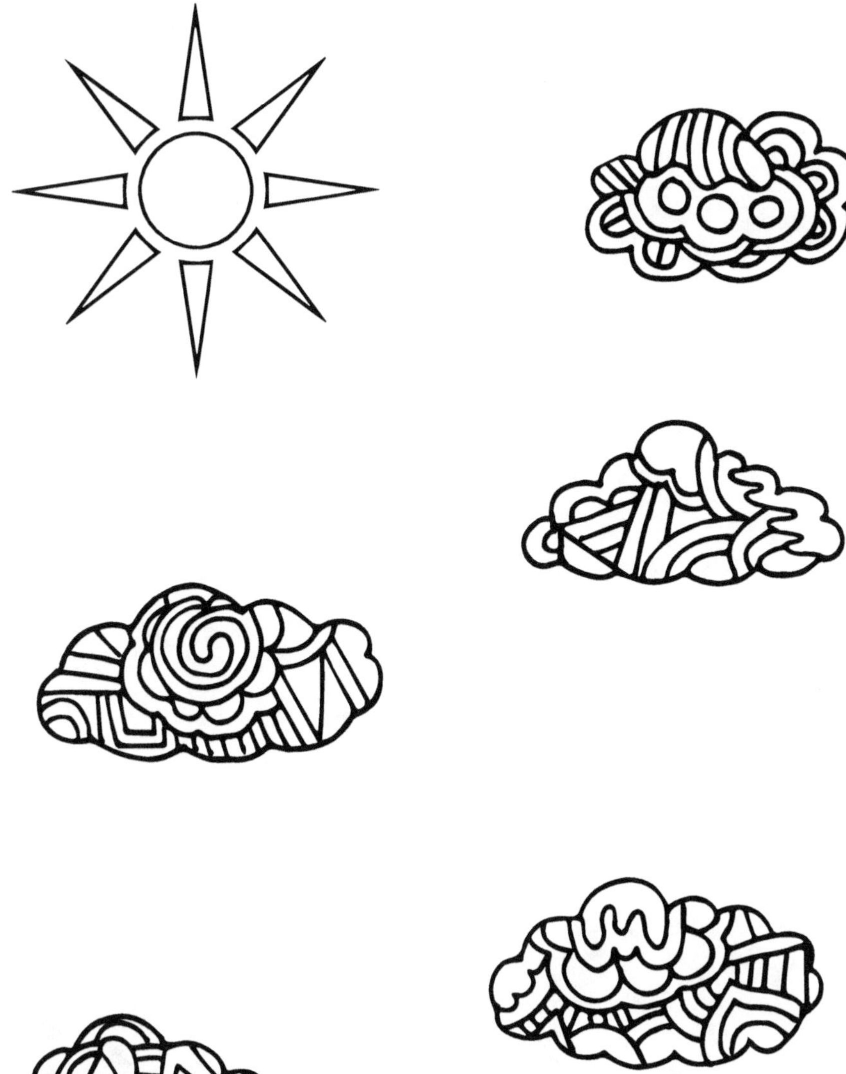

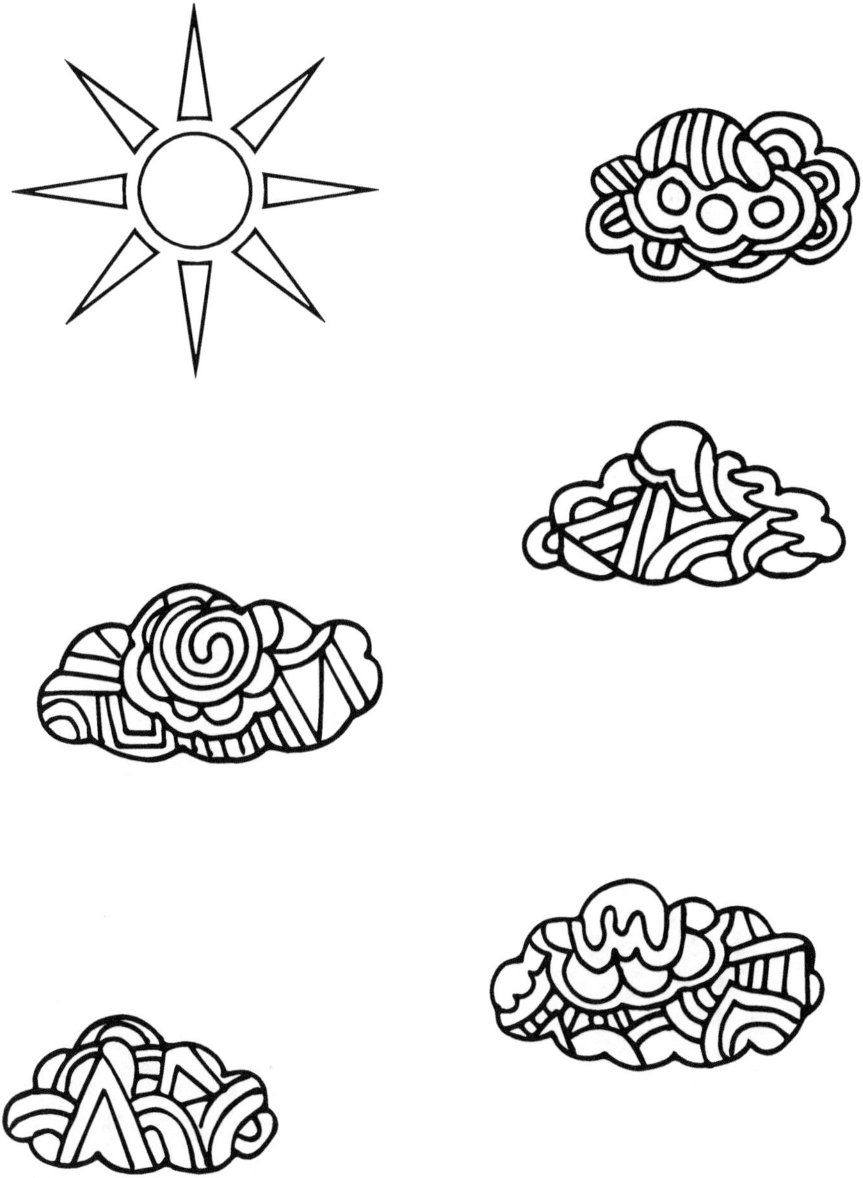

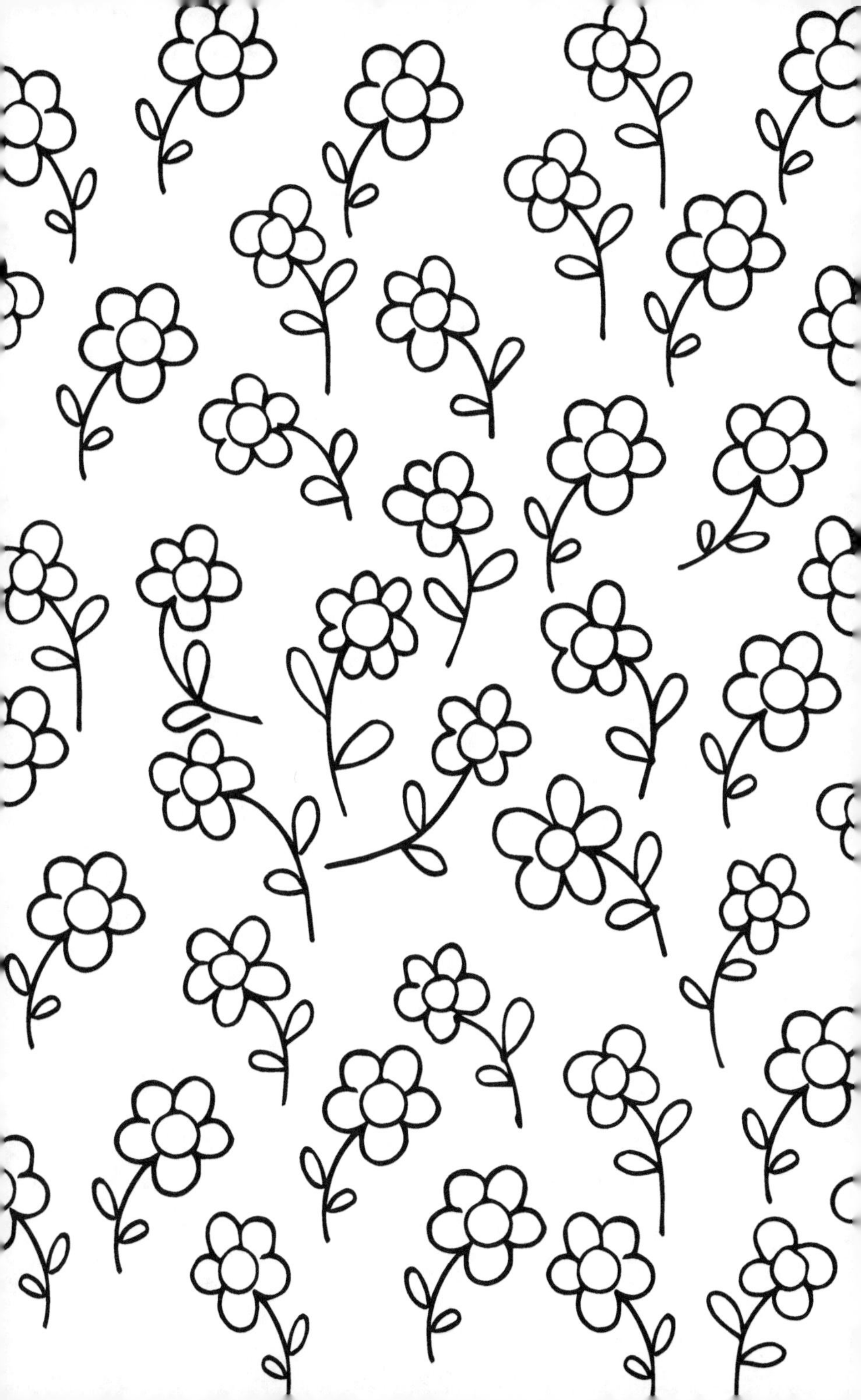

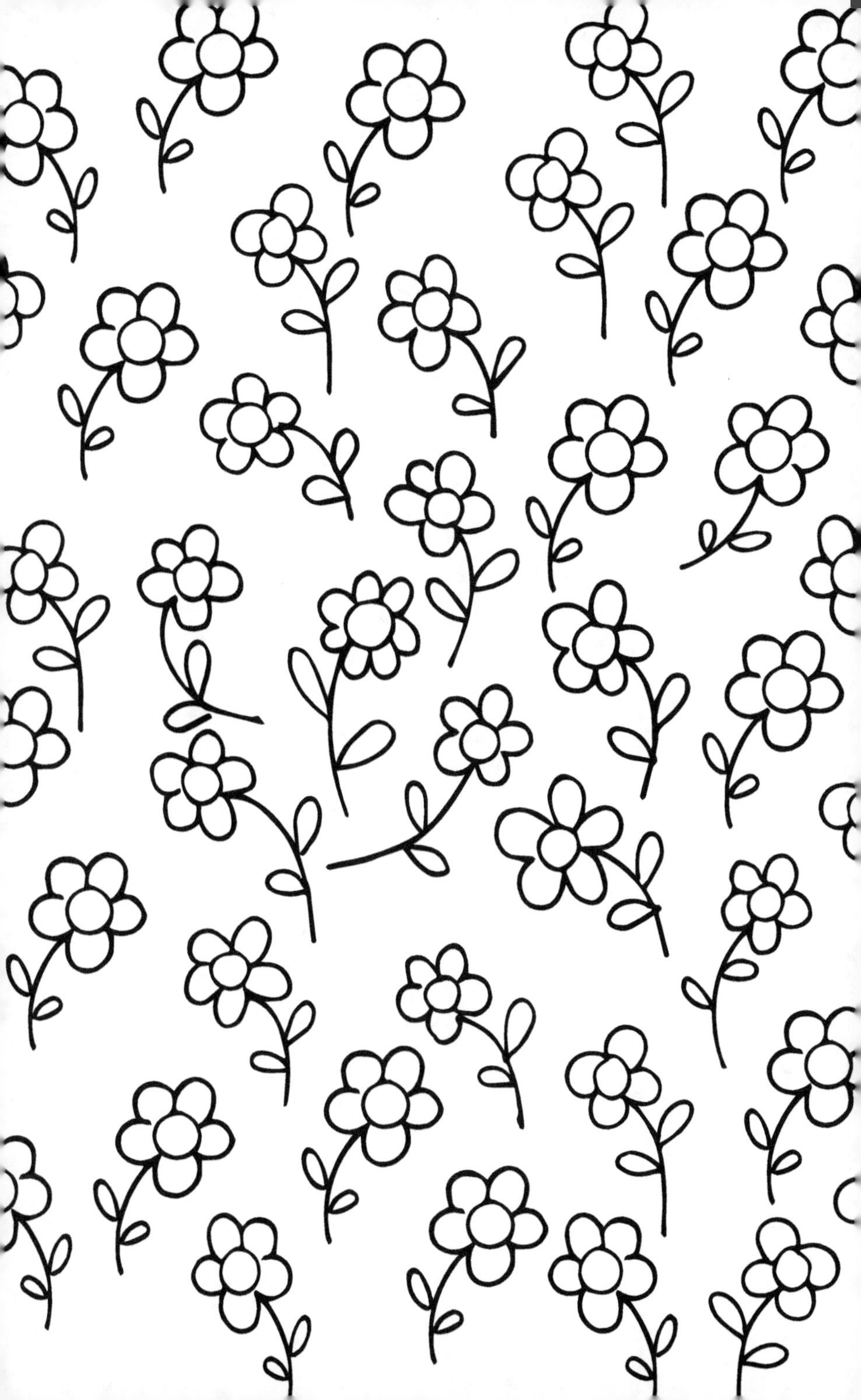

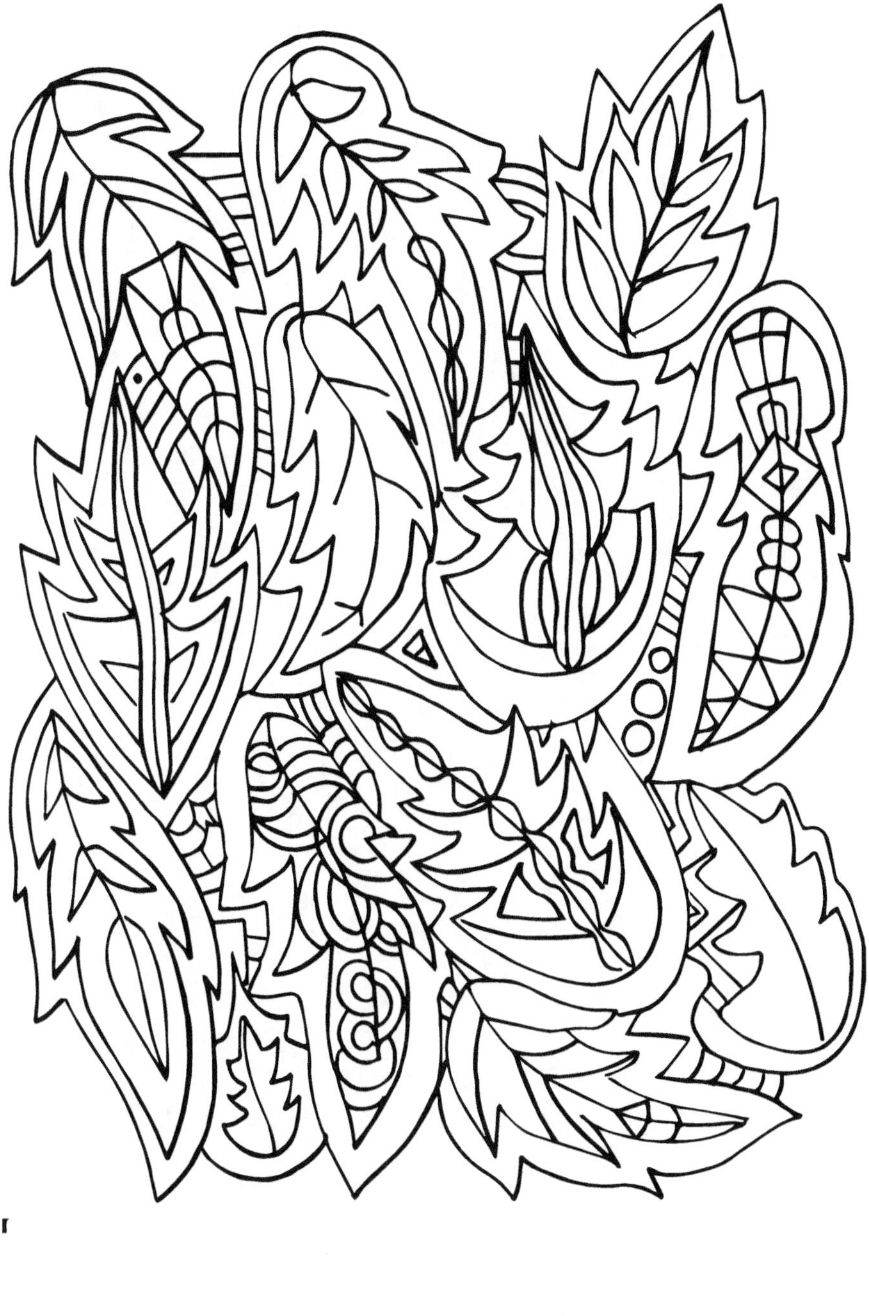

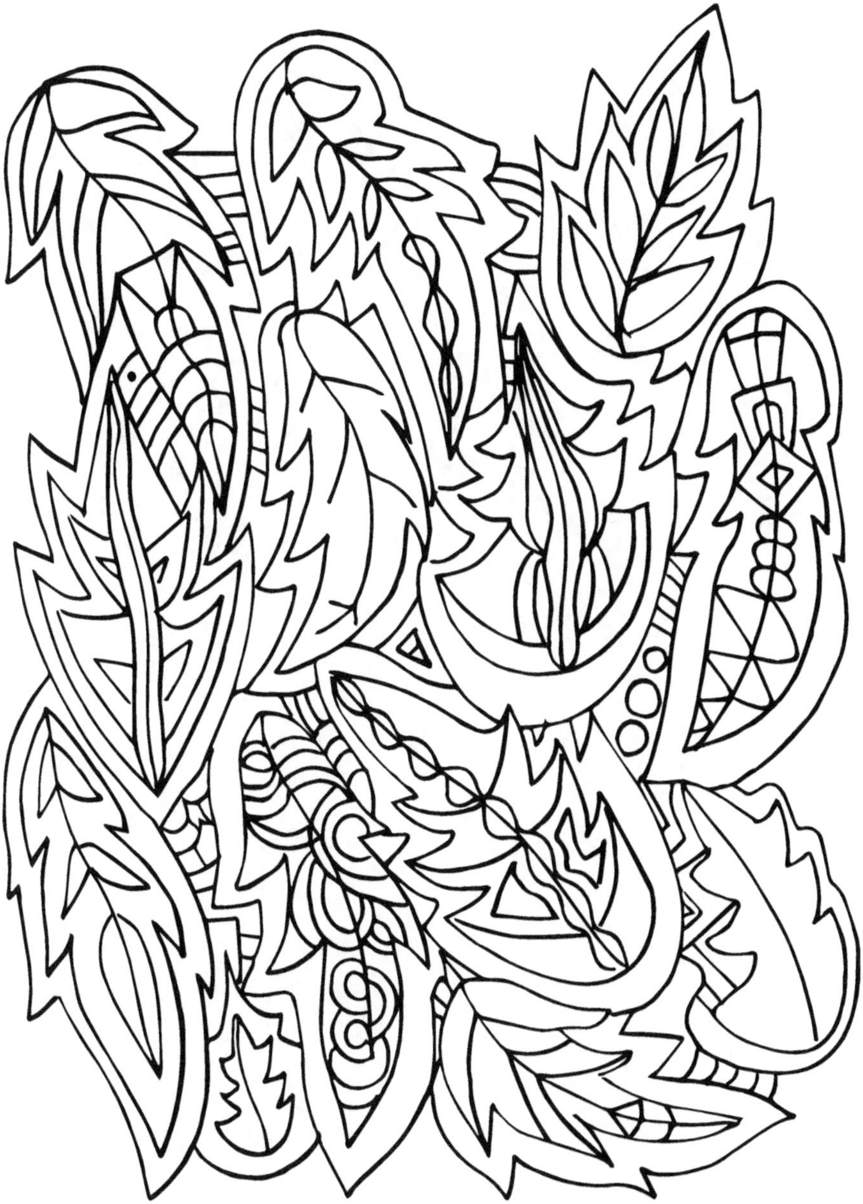

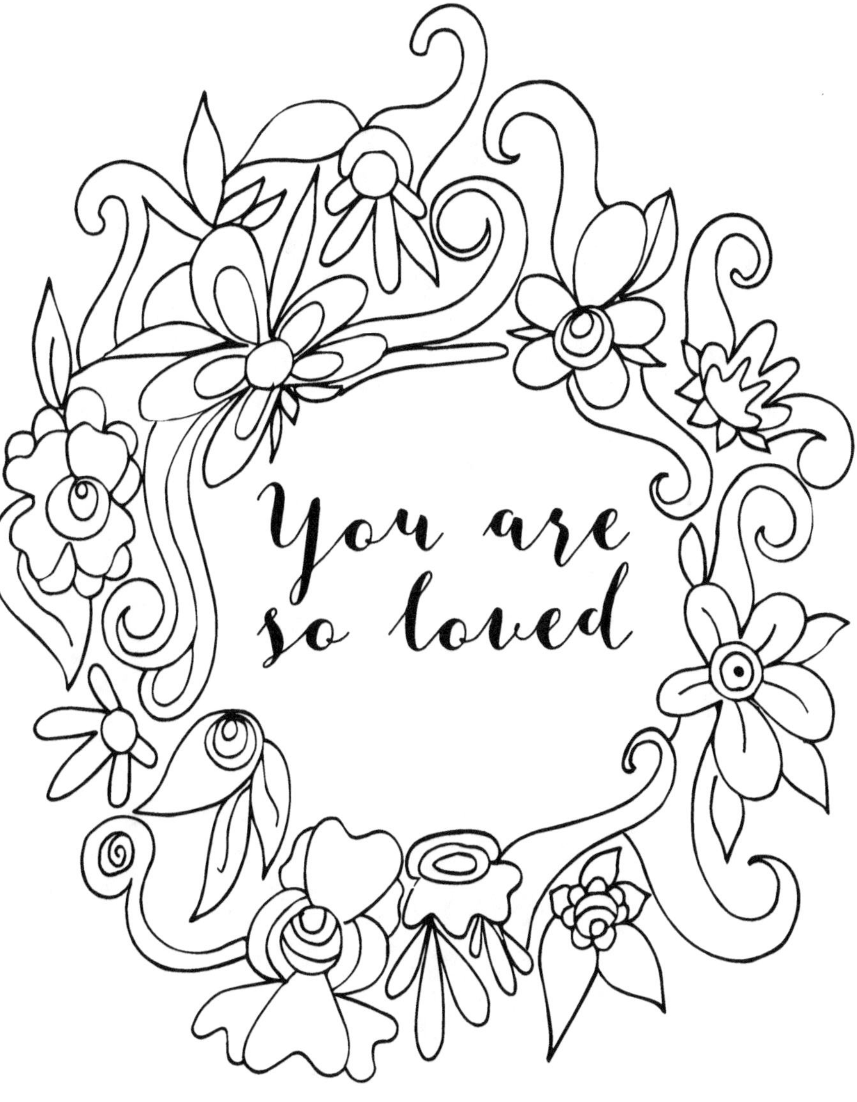
You are
so loved

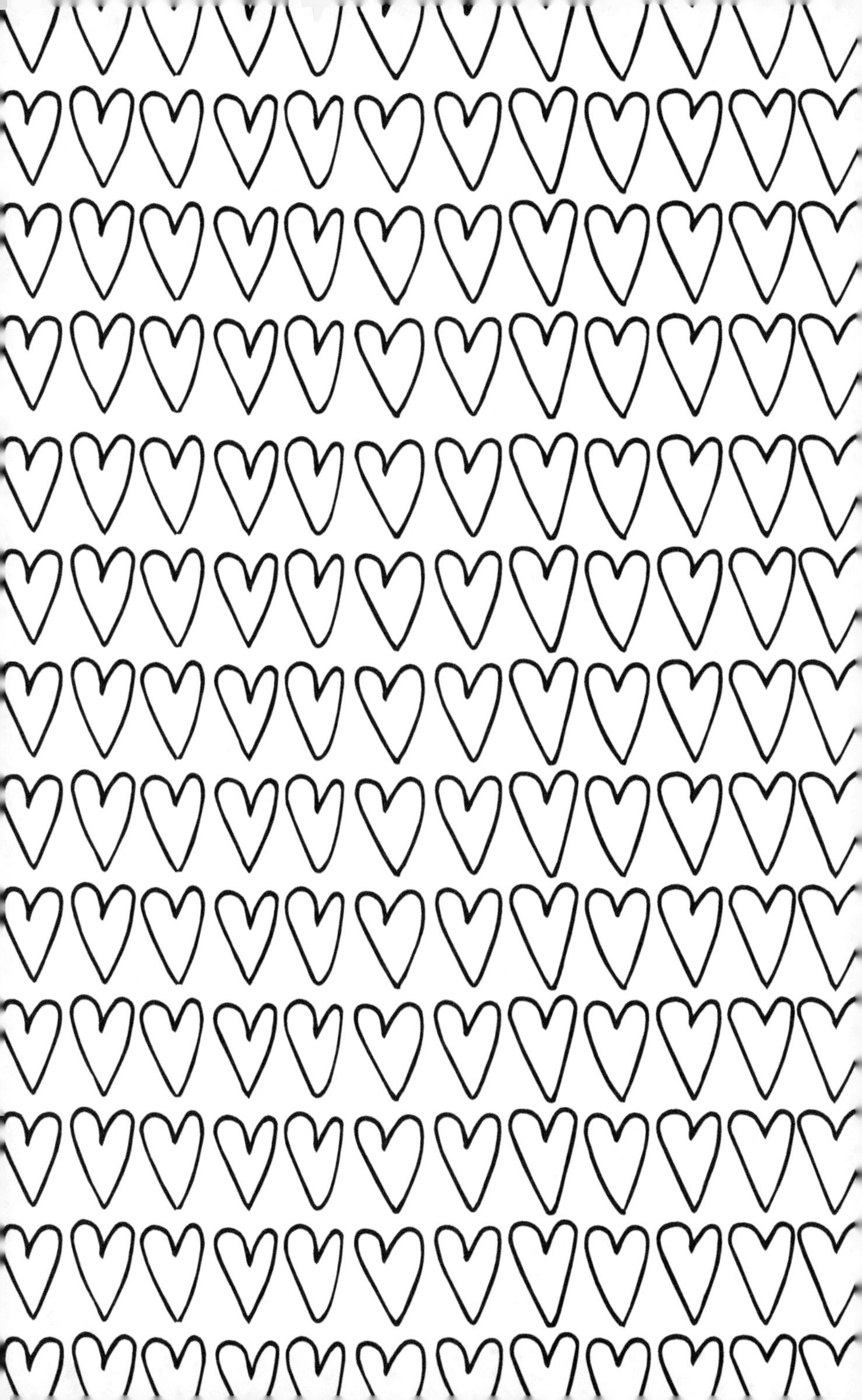

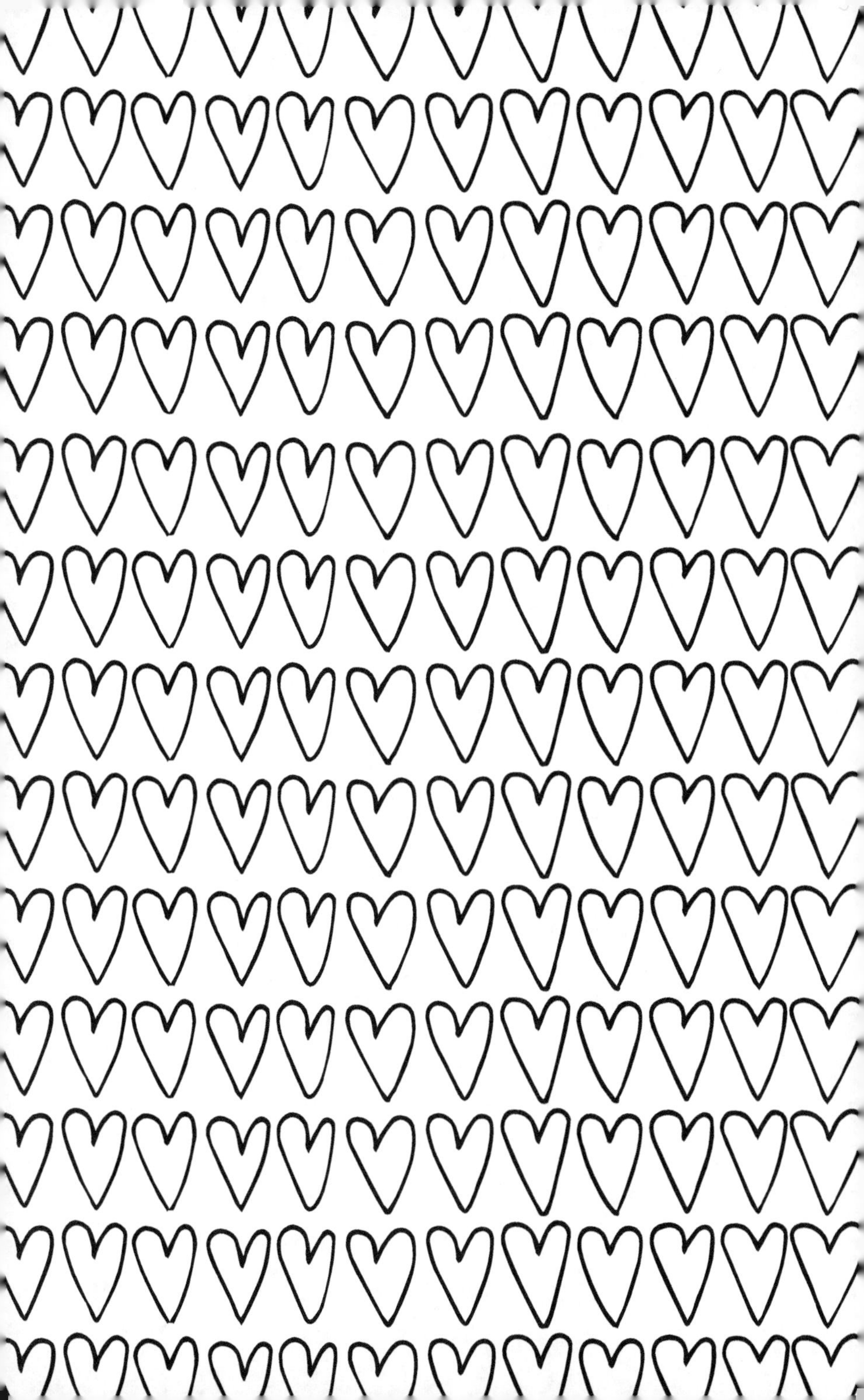

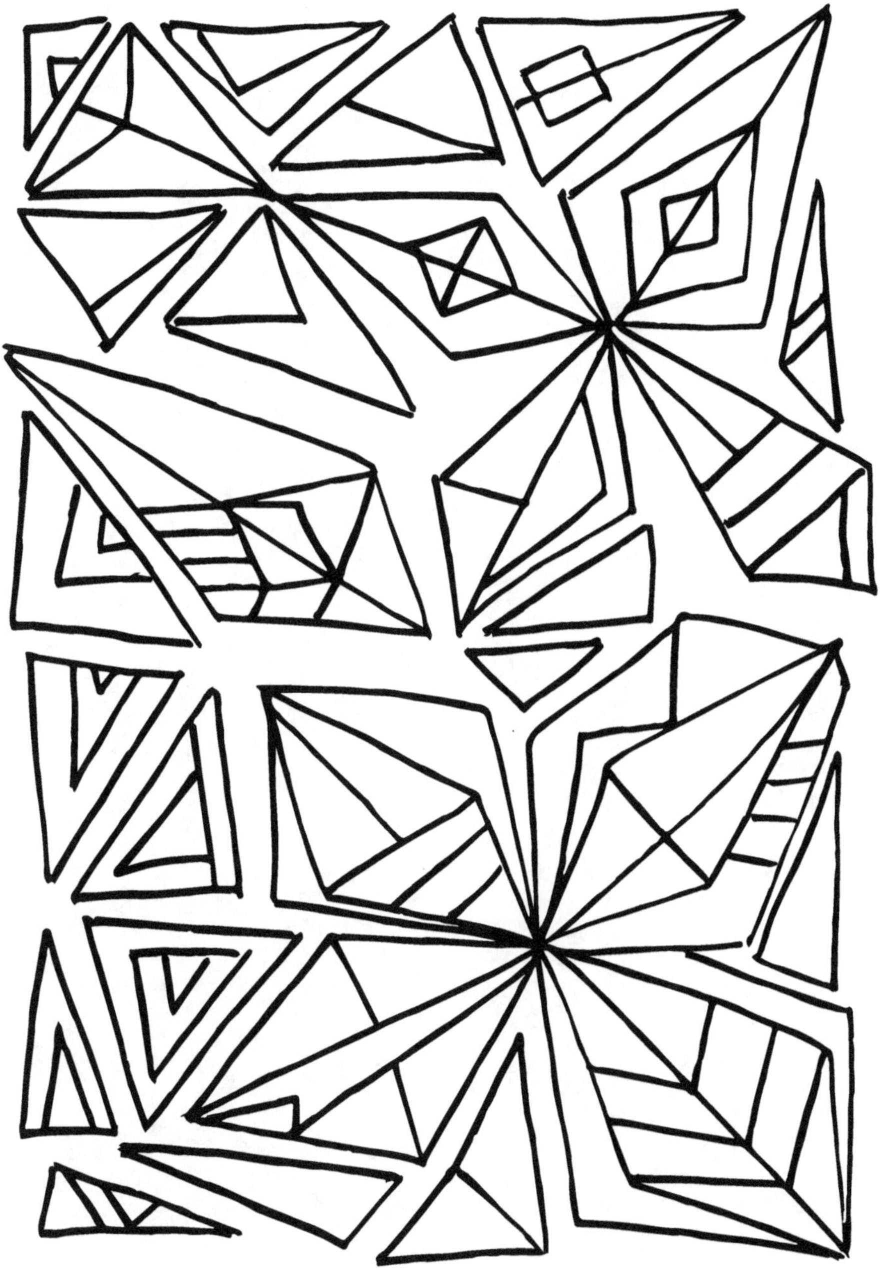

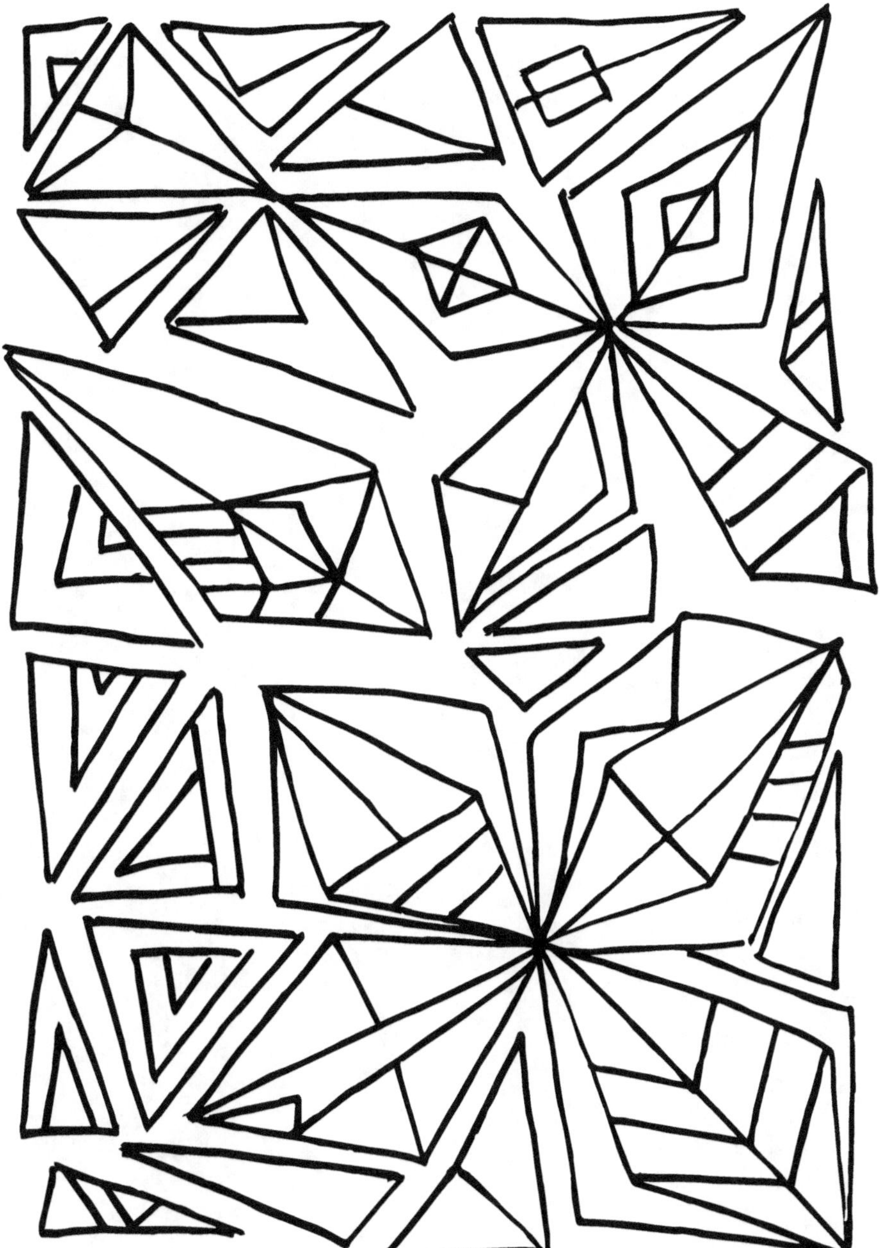

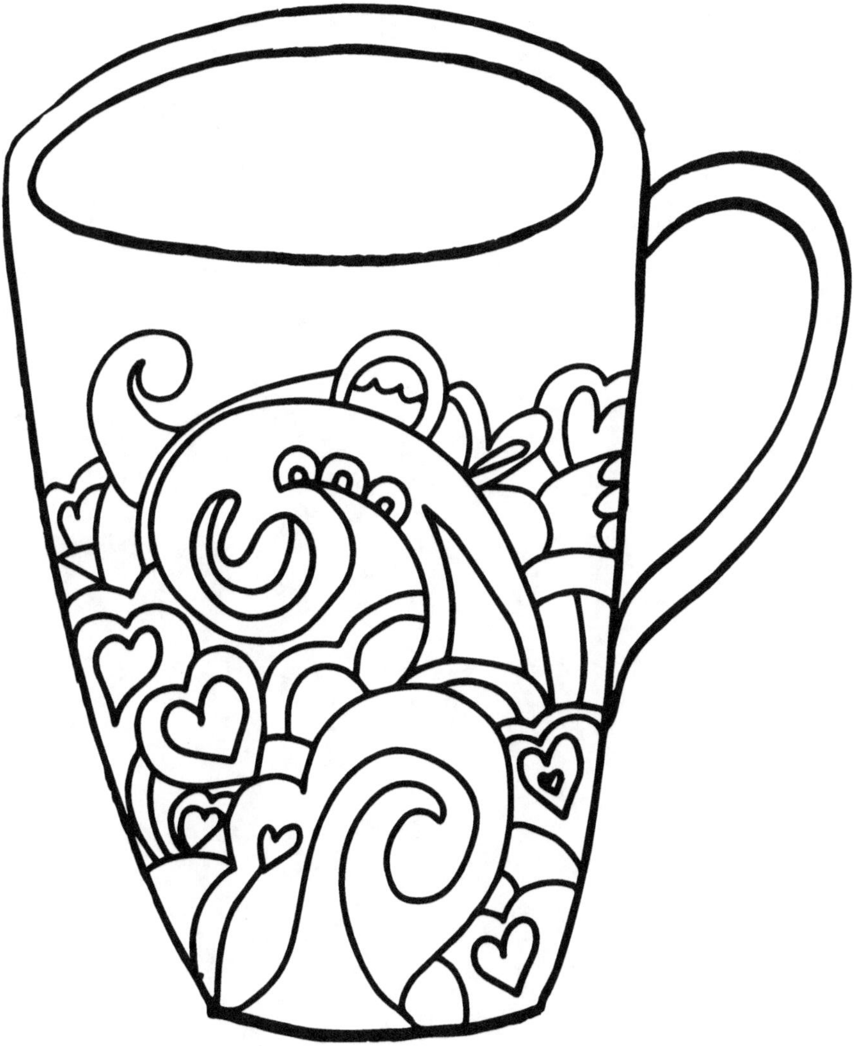

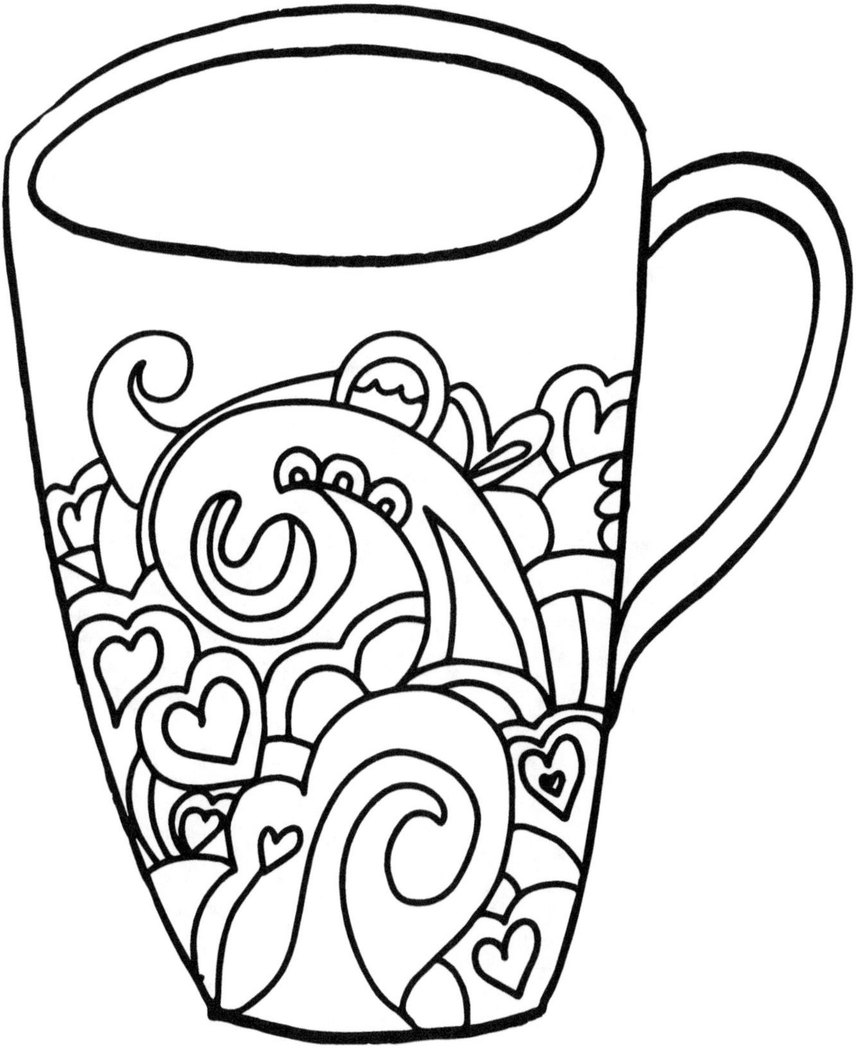

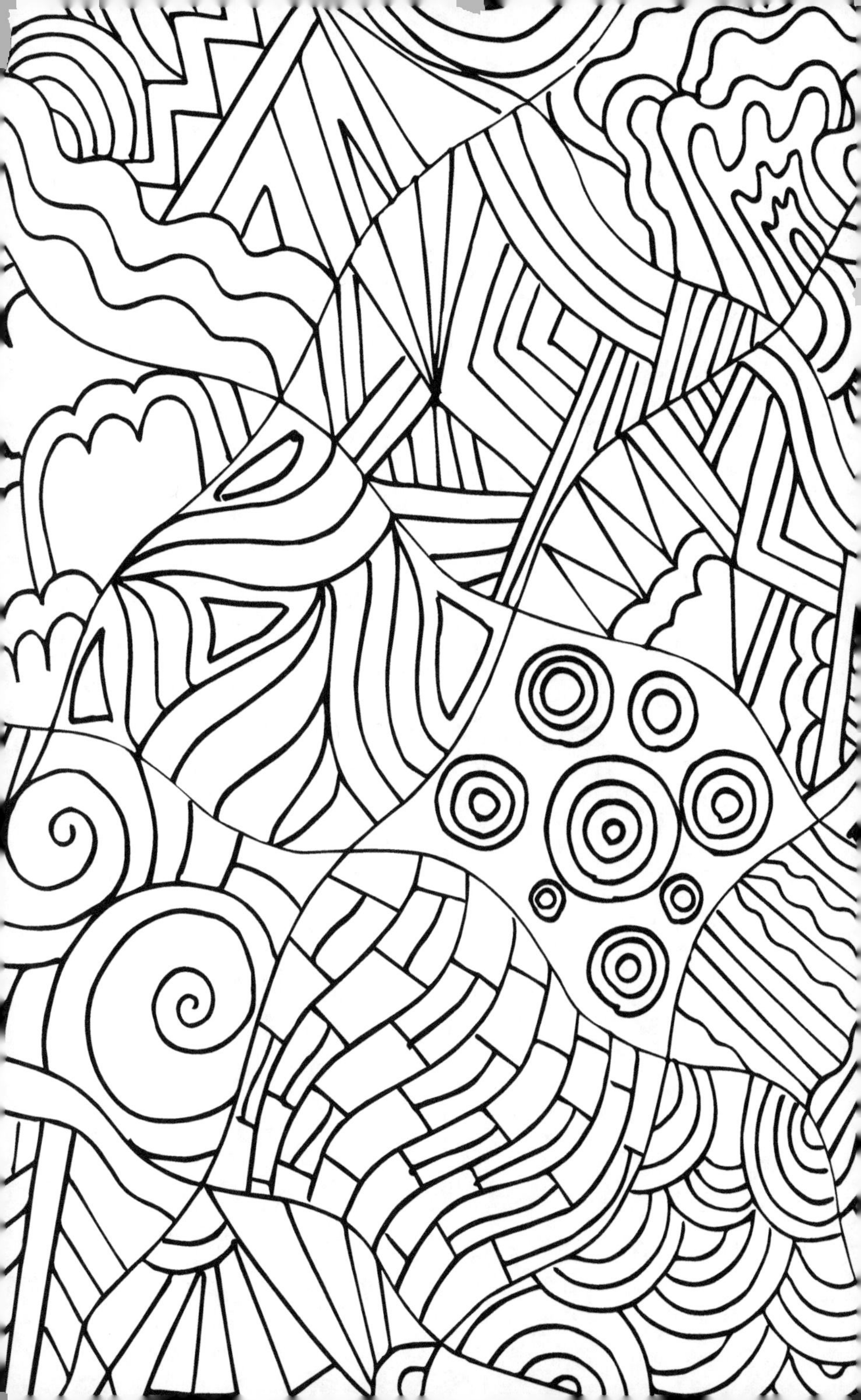

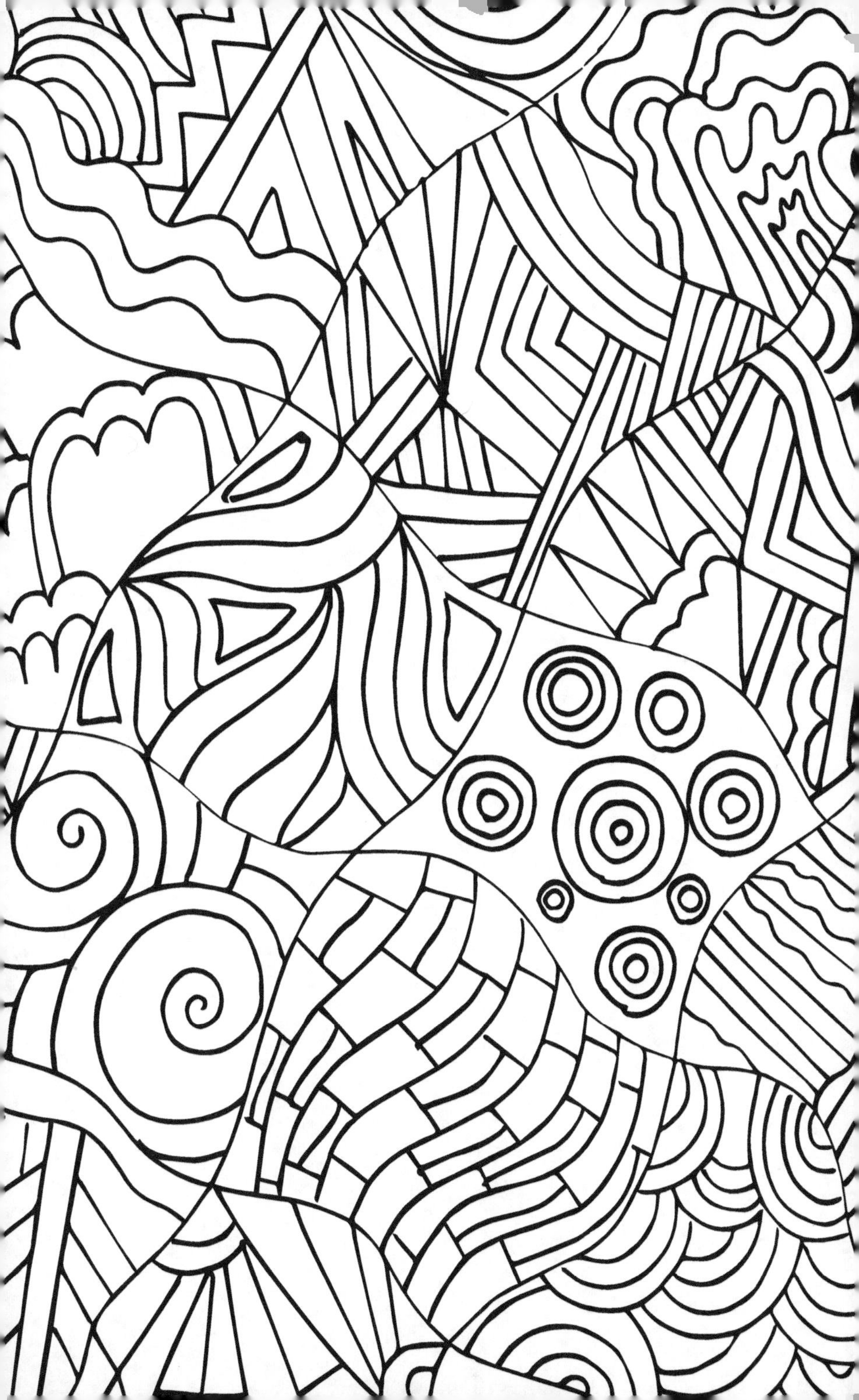

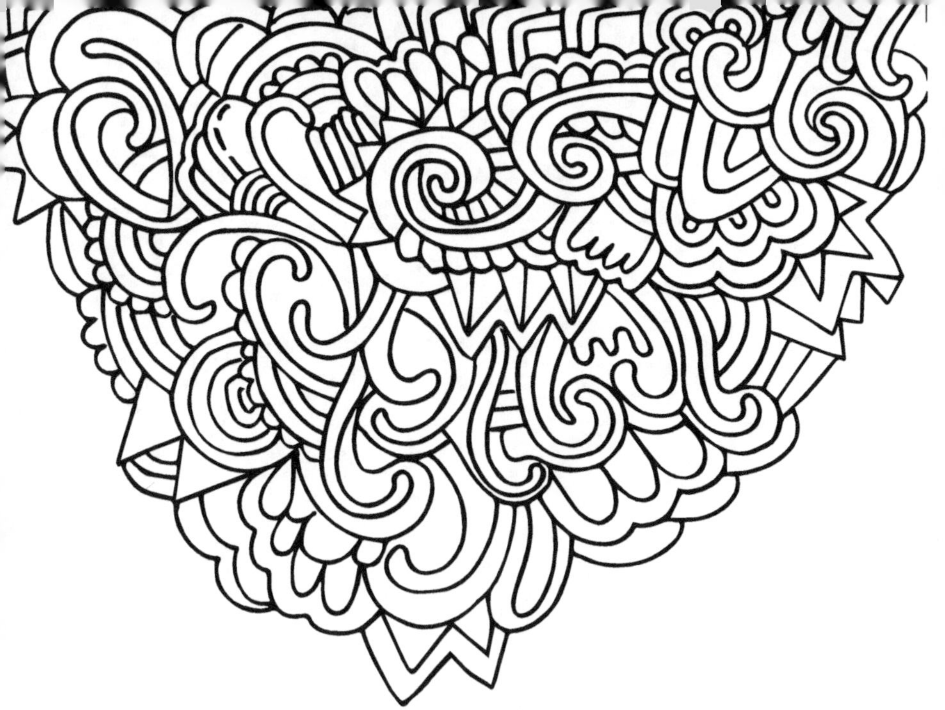

Love your body

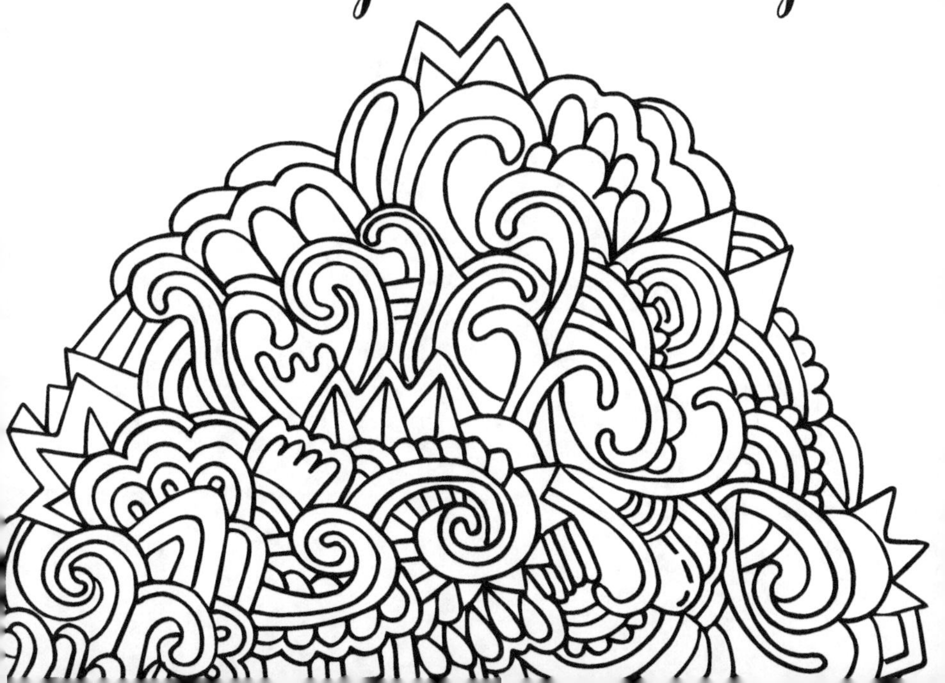

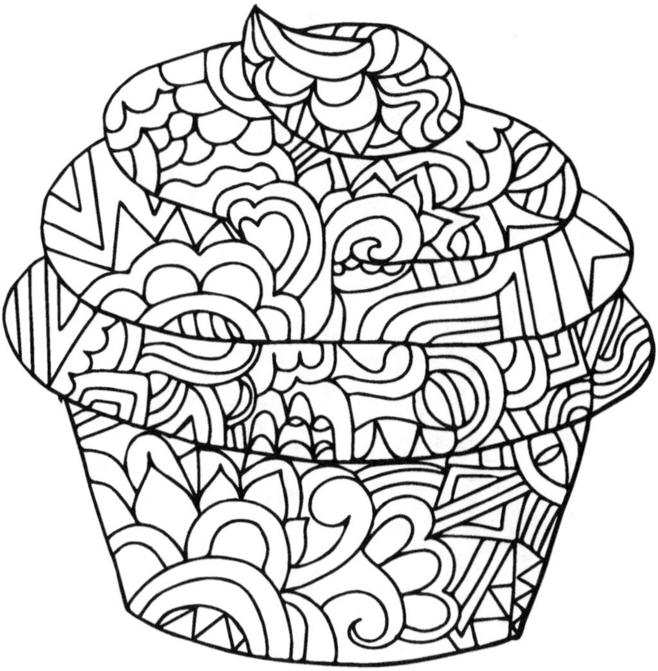

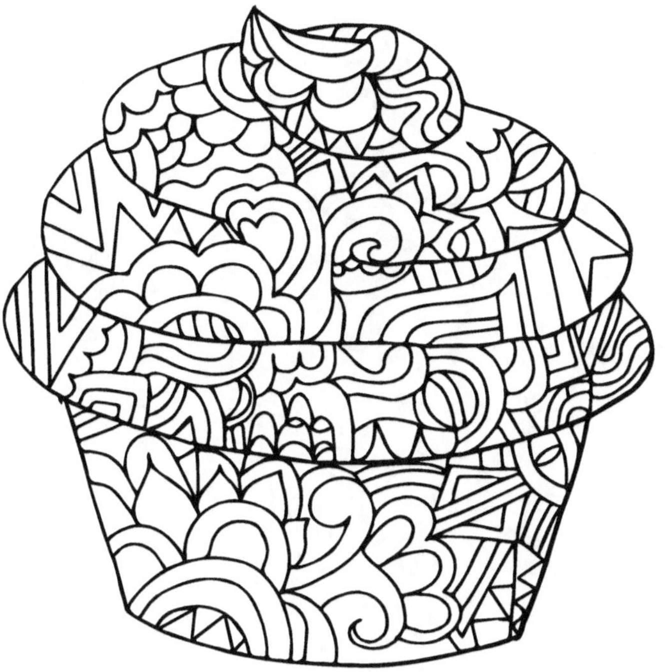

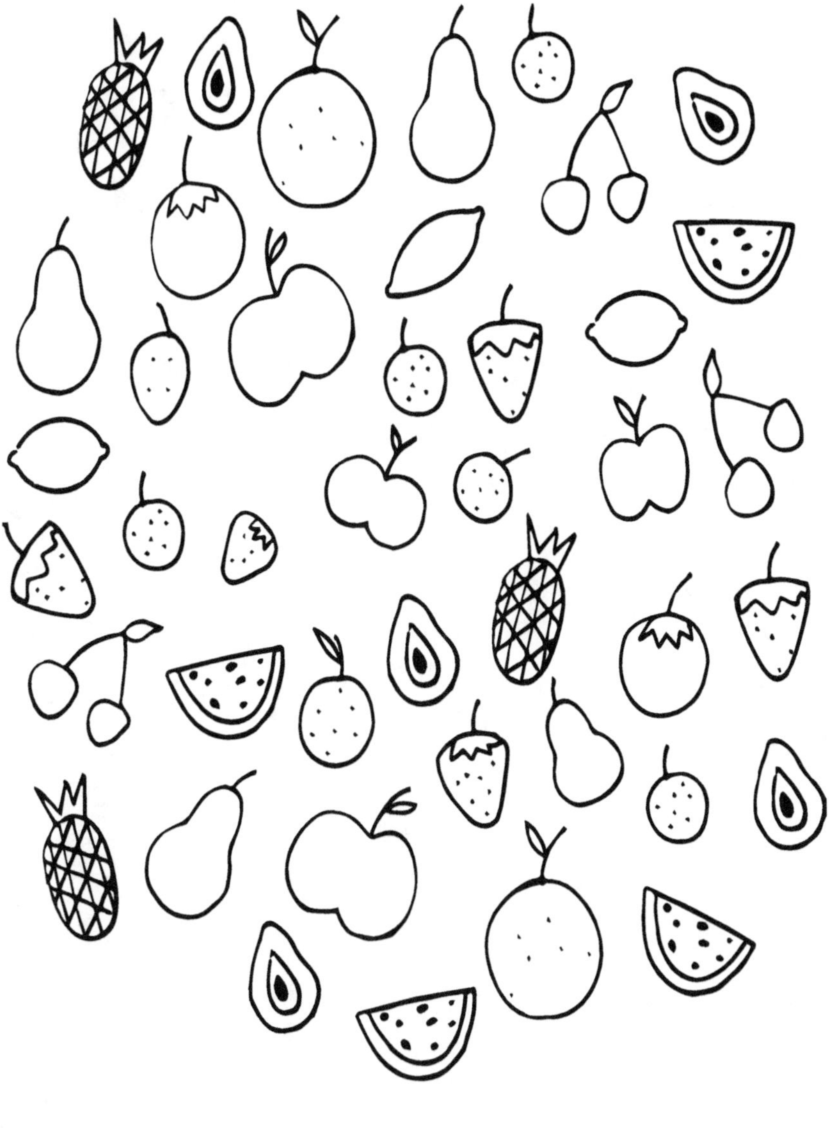

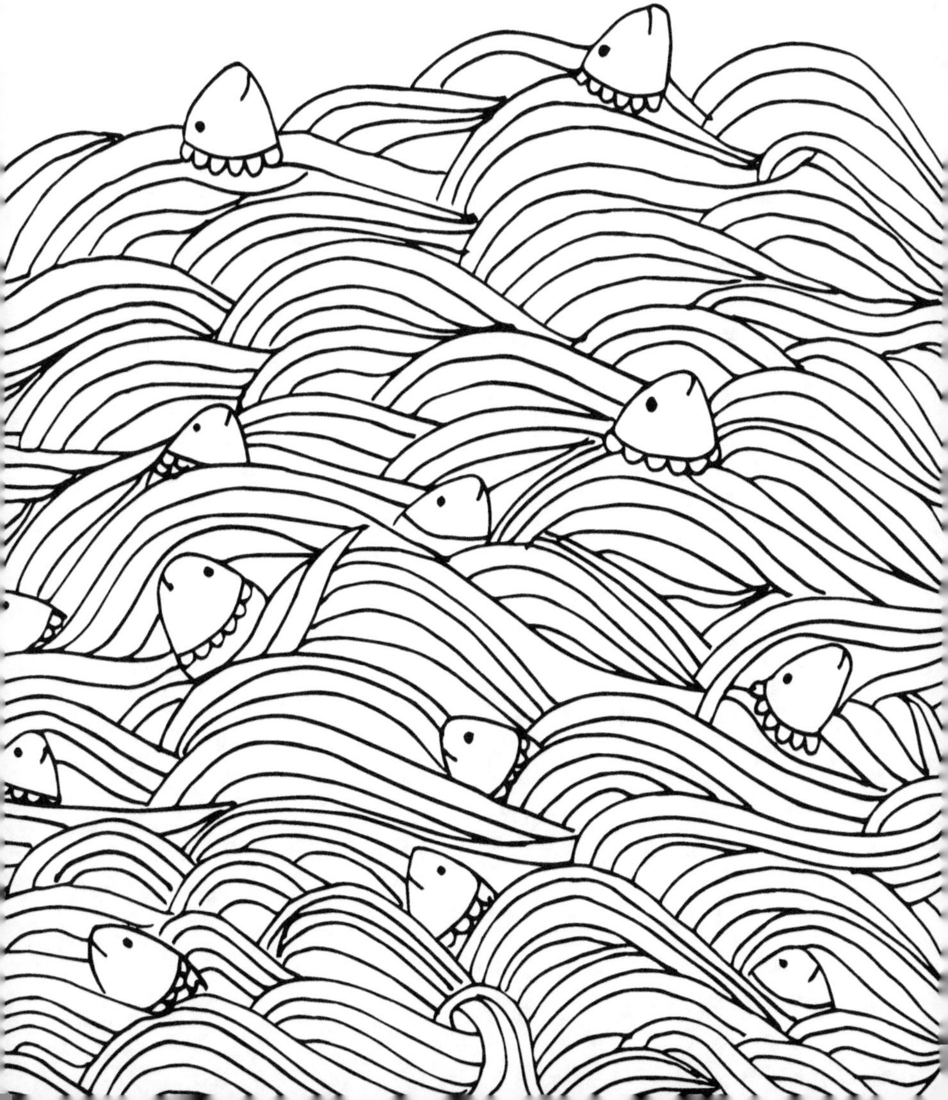

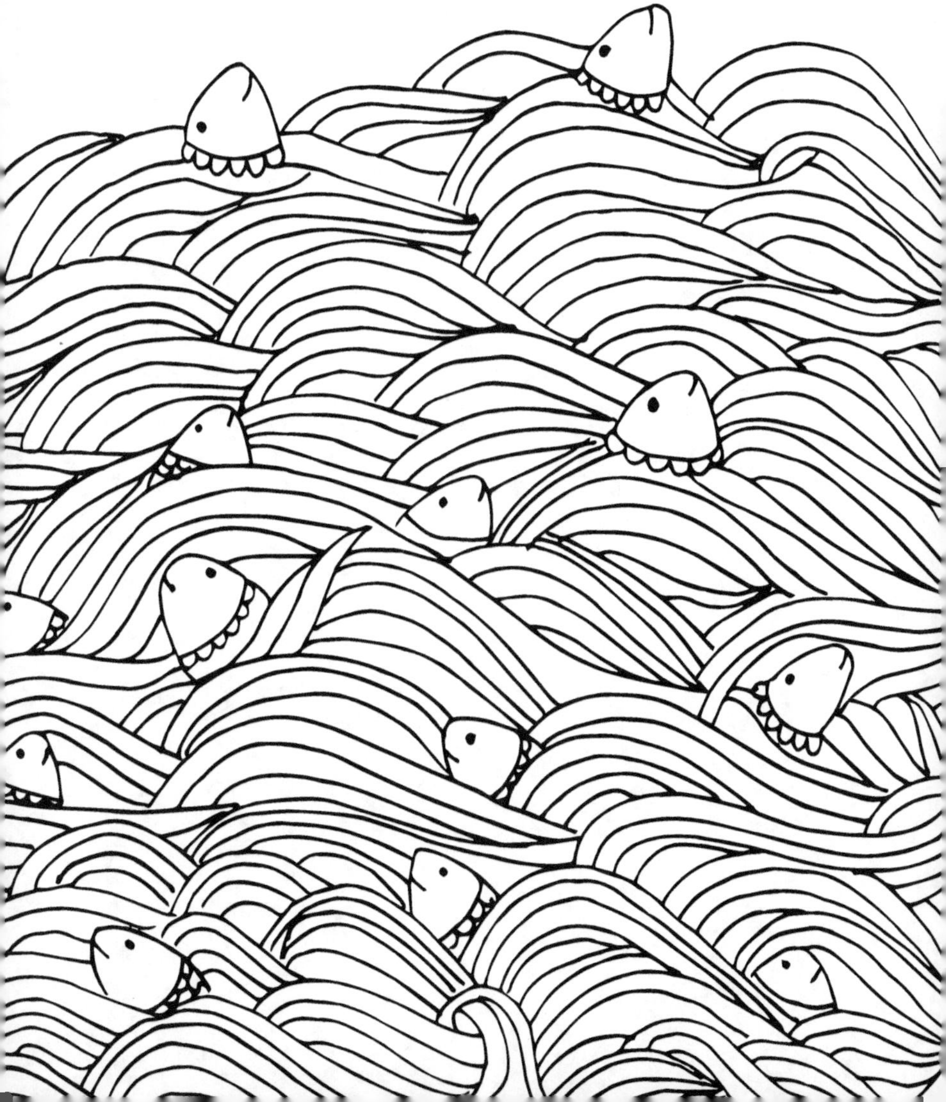

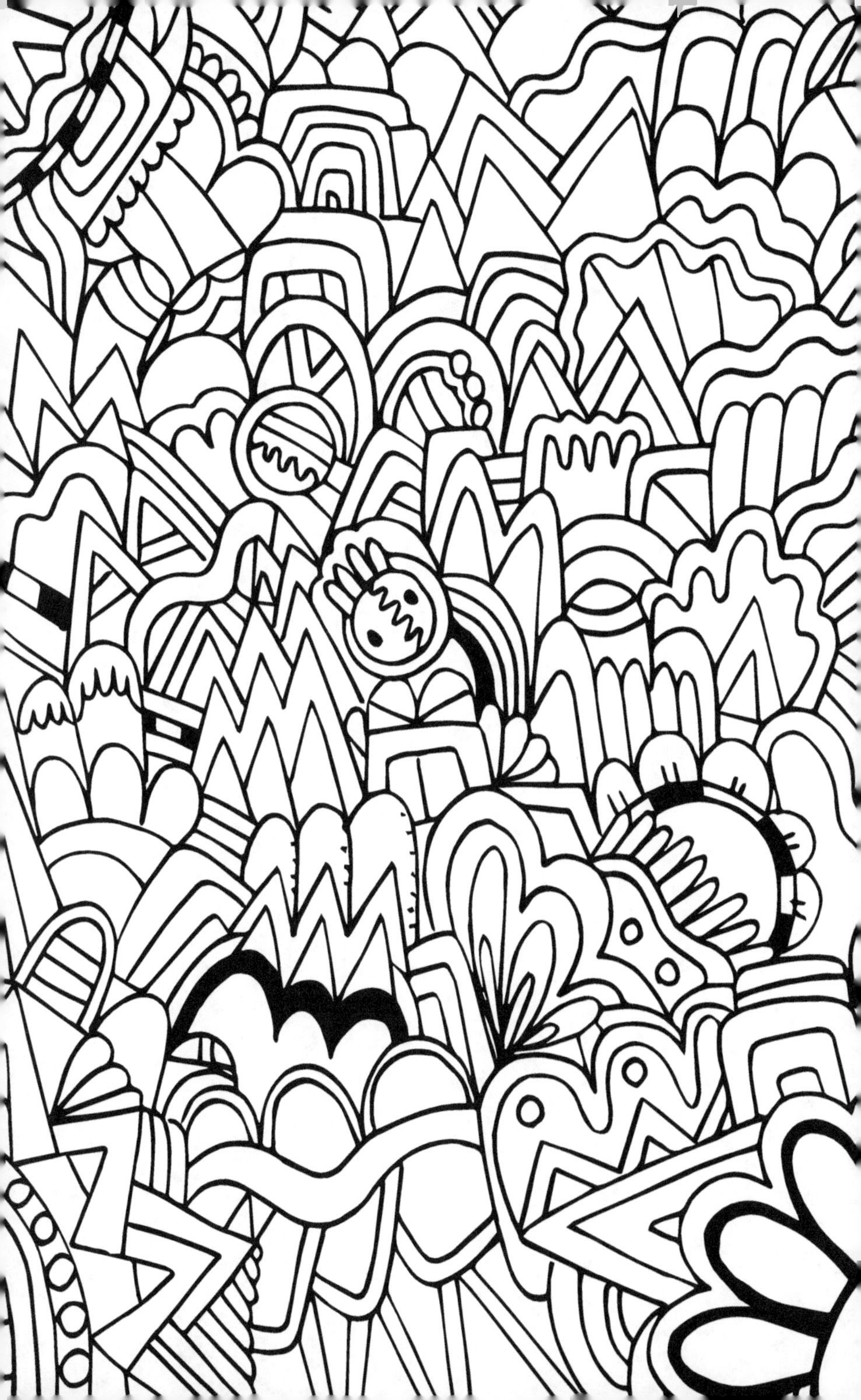

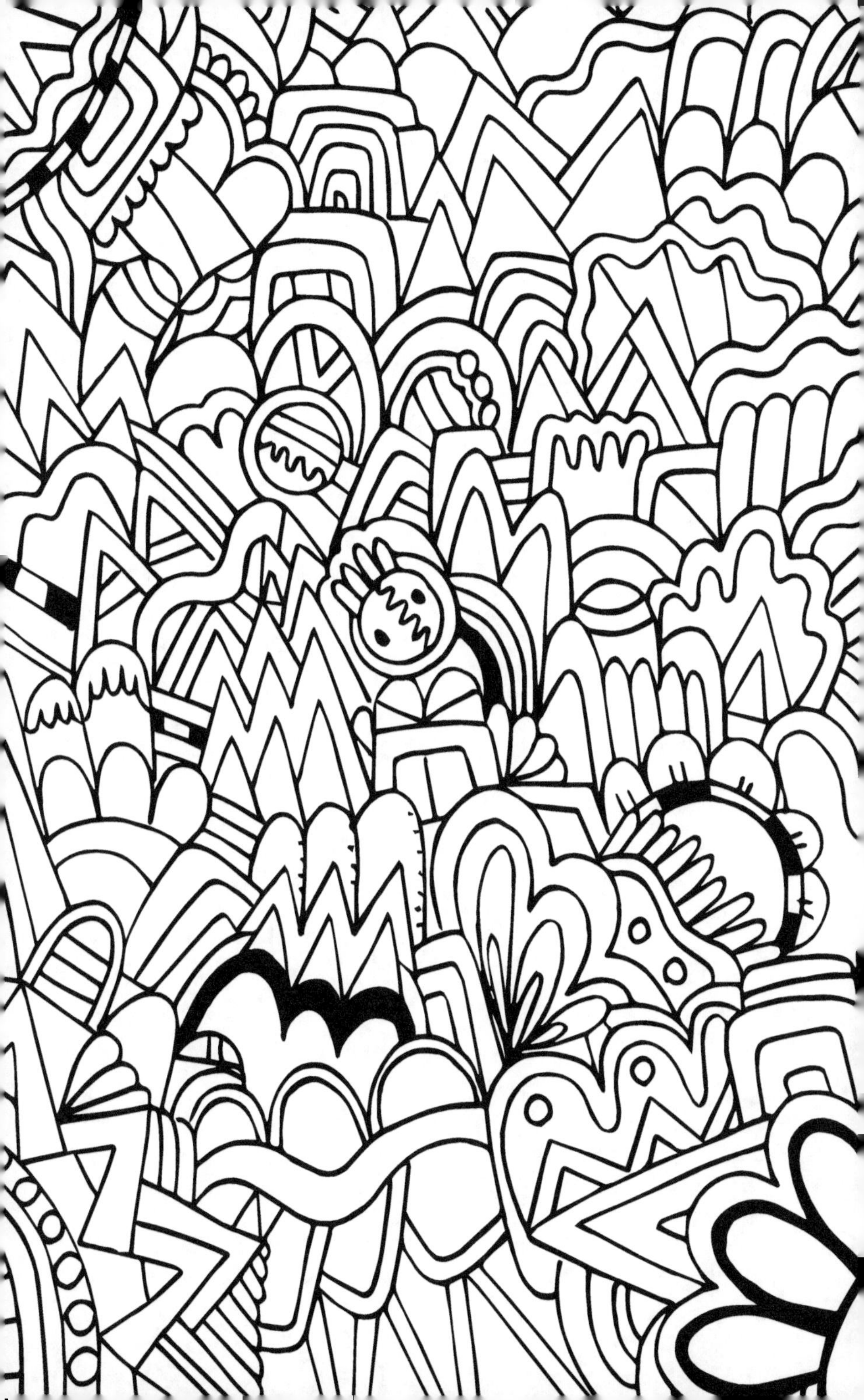

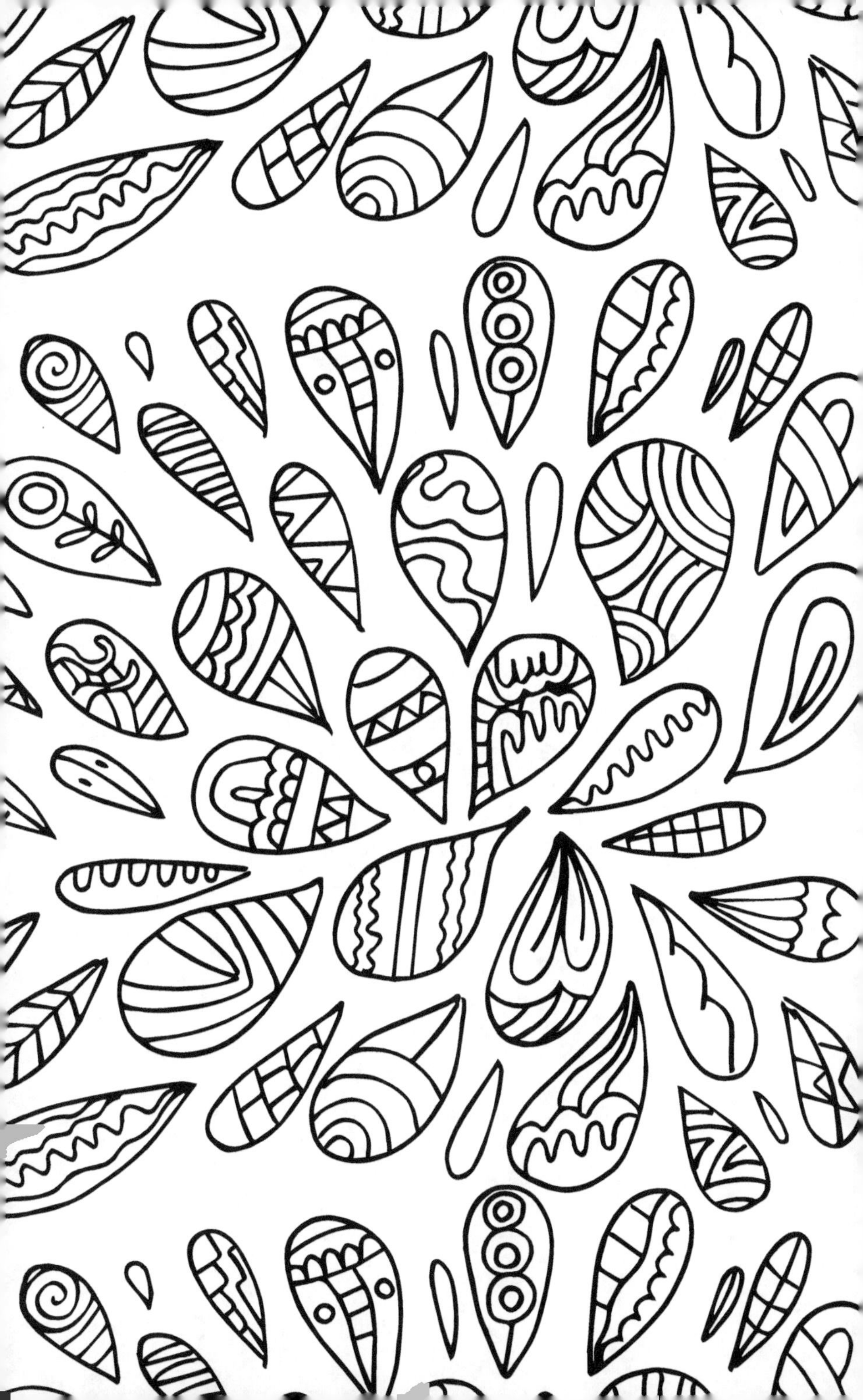

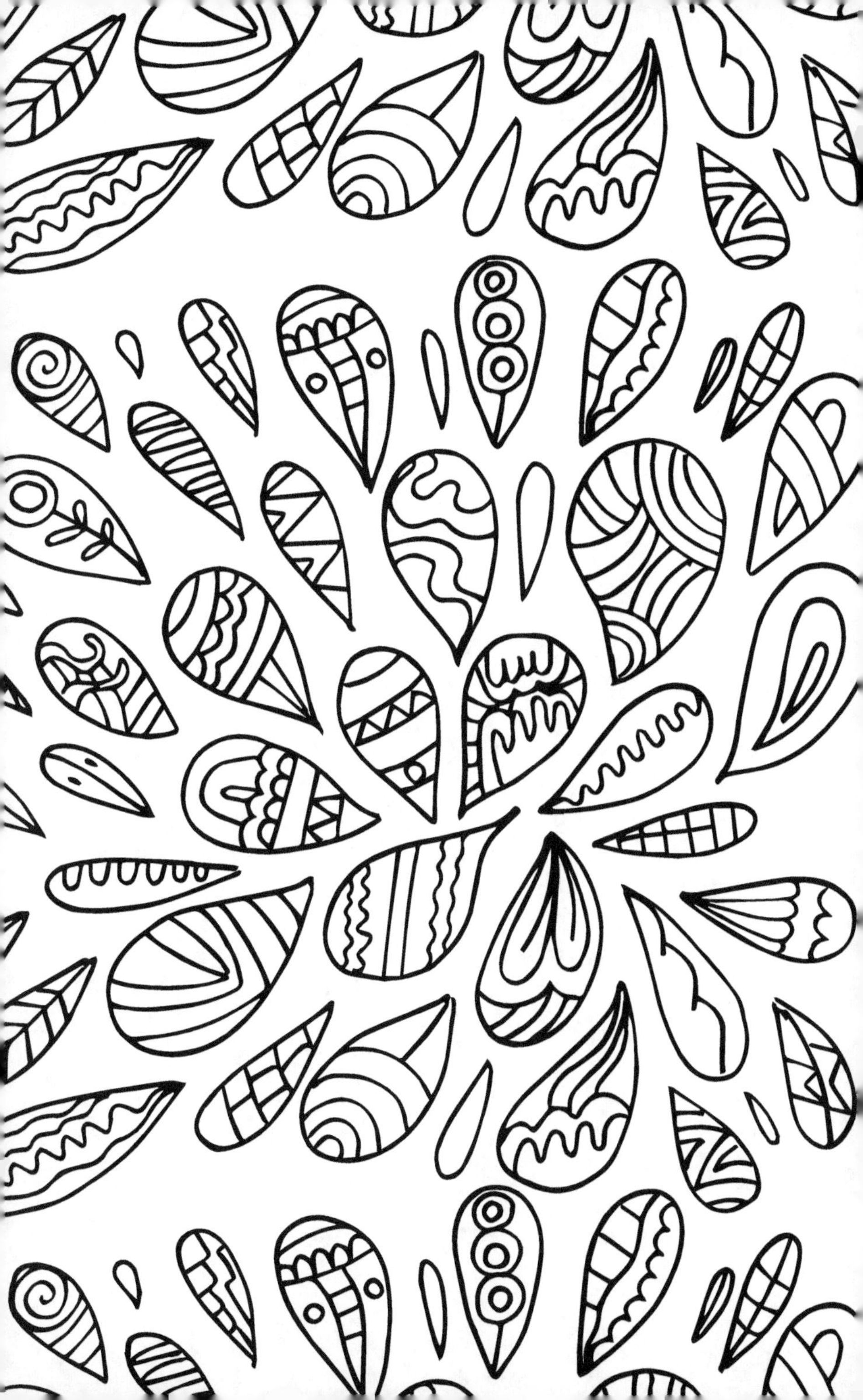

You are ENOUGH

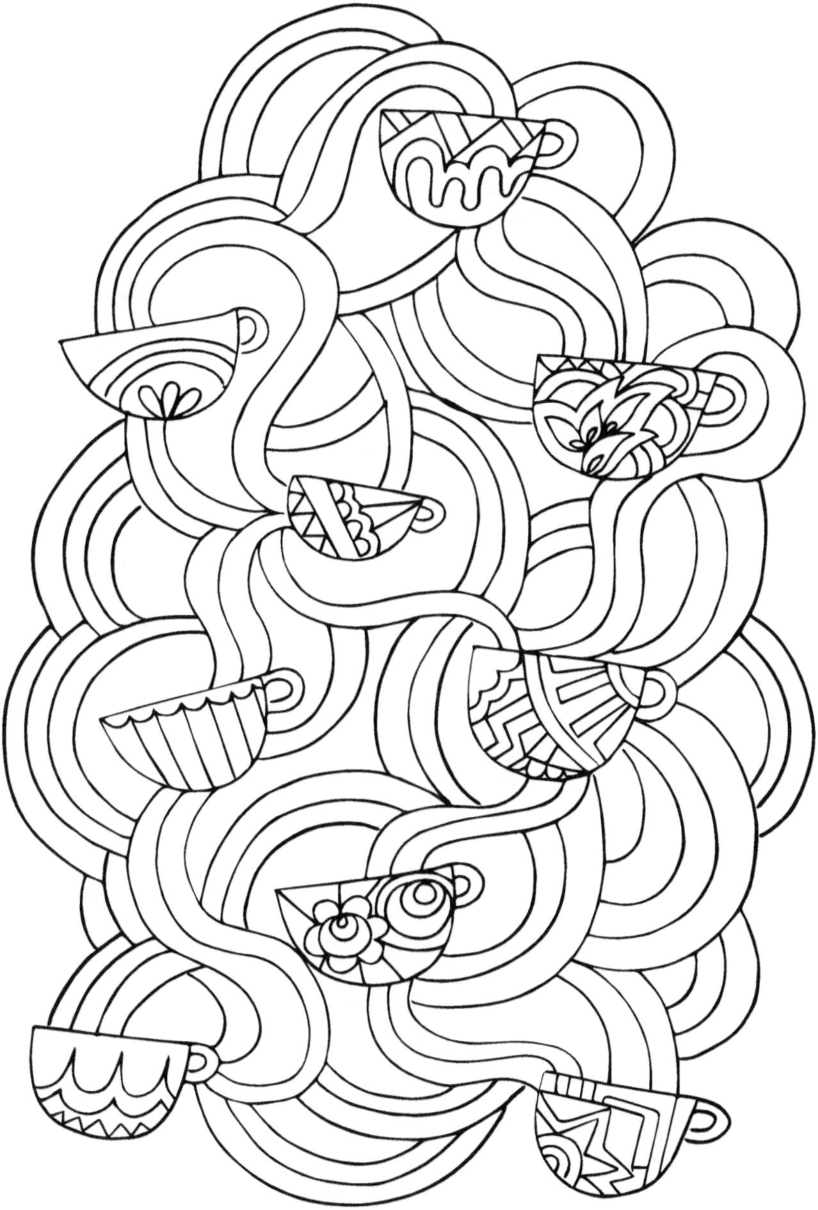

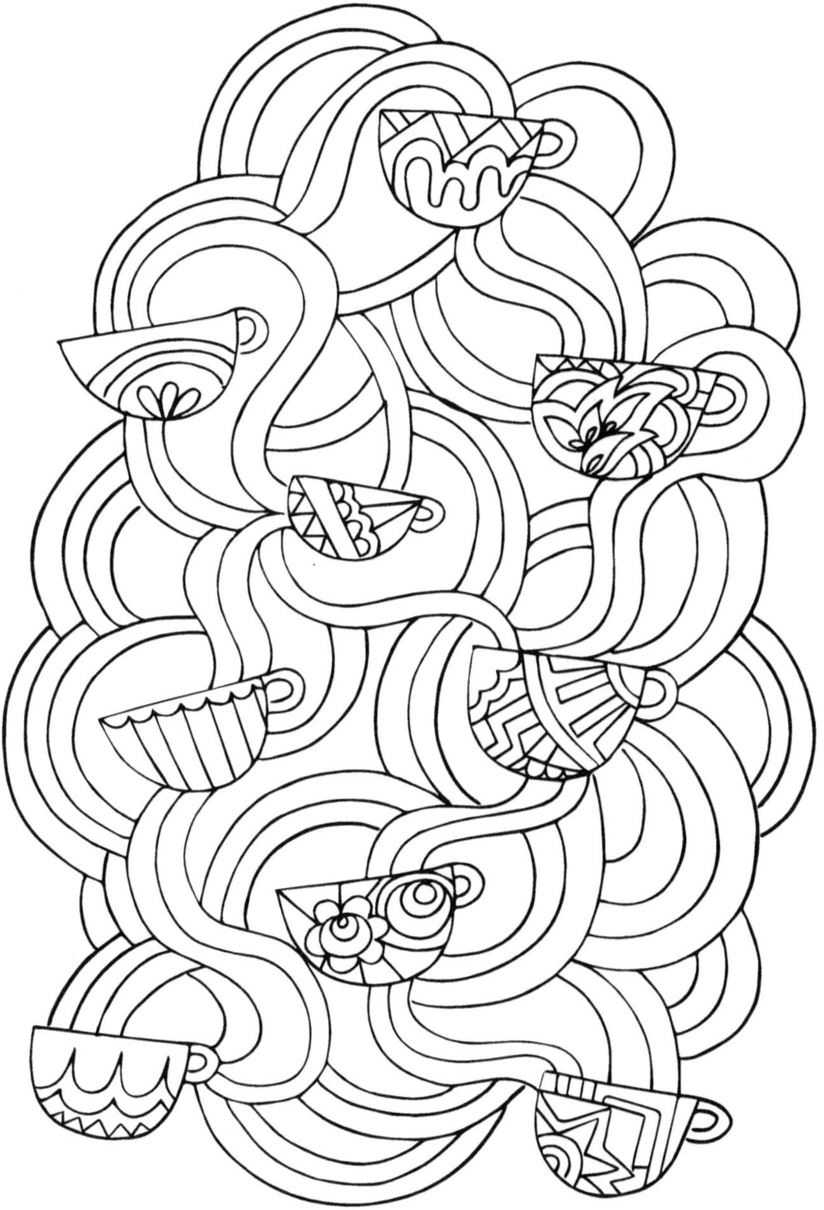

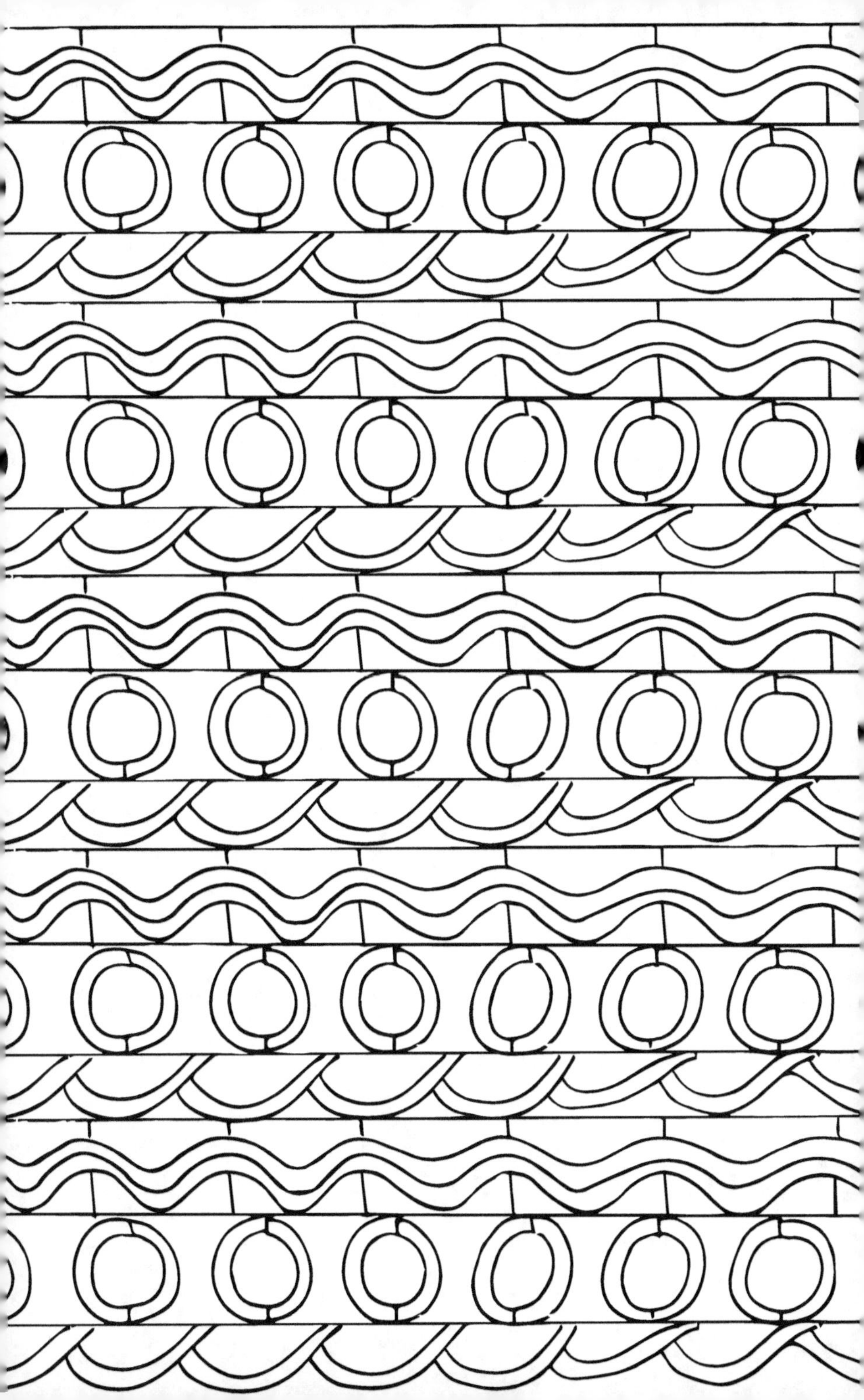

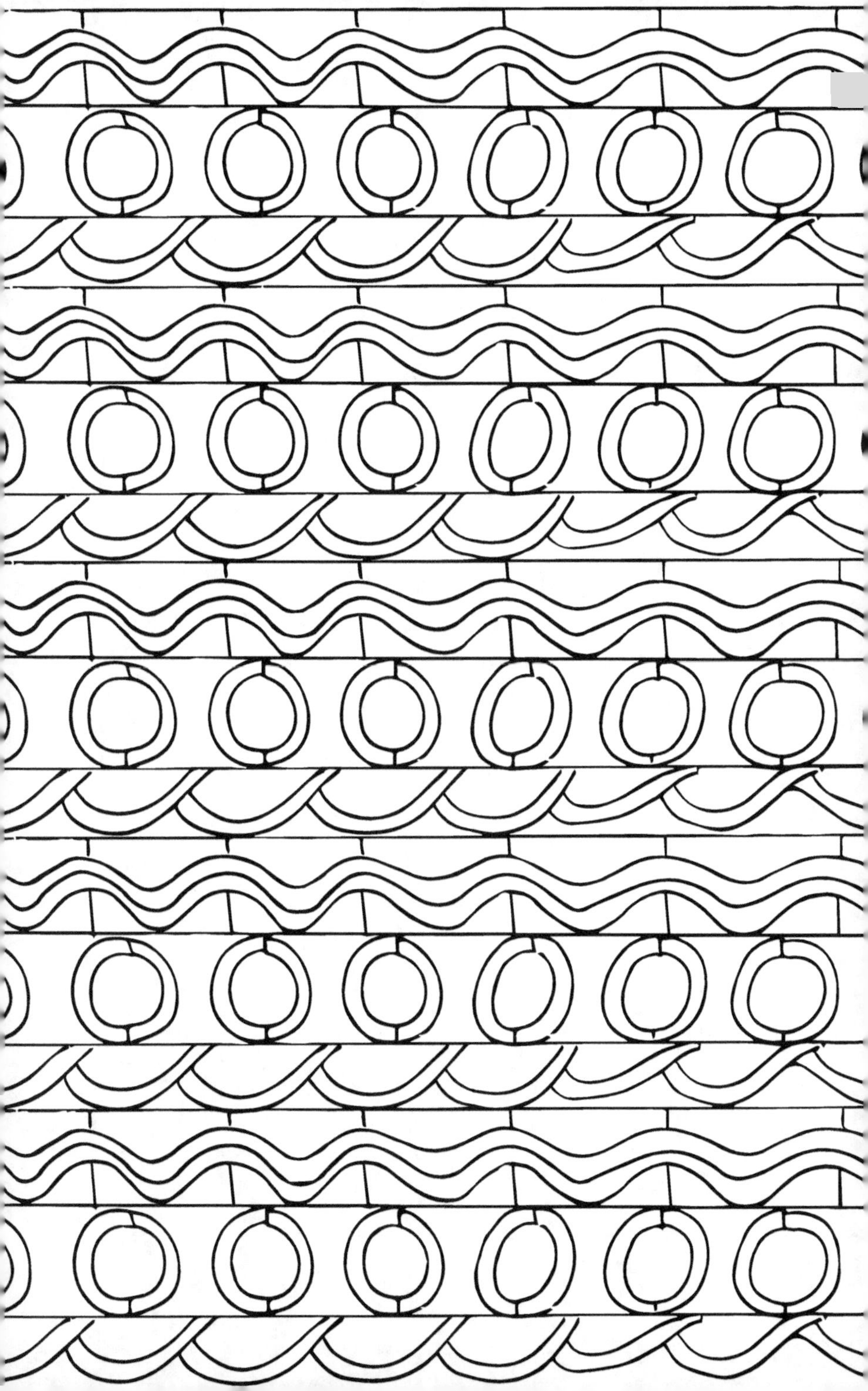

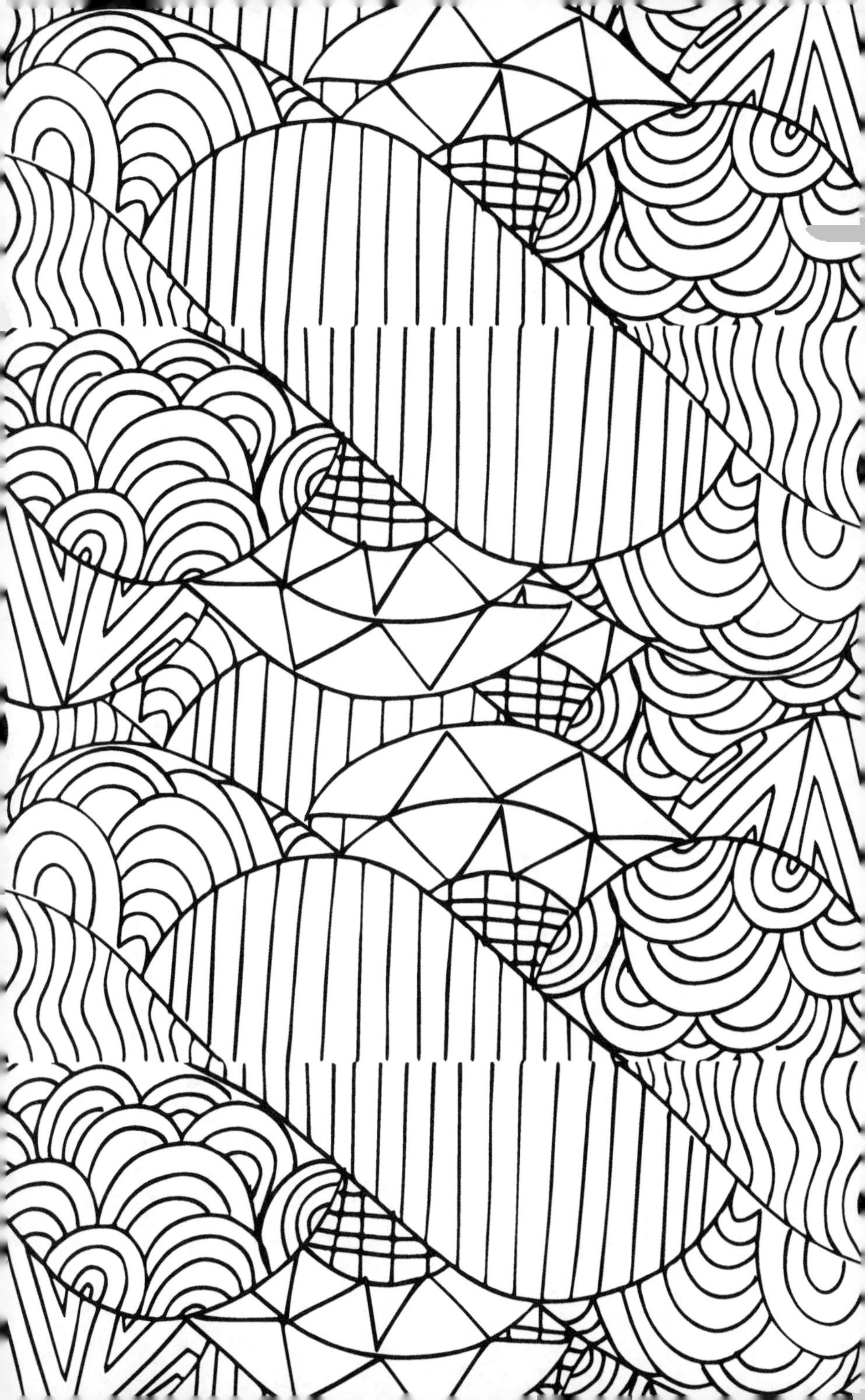

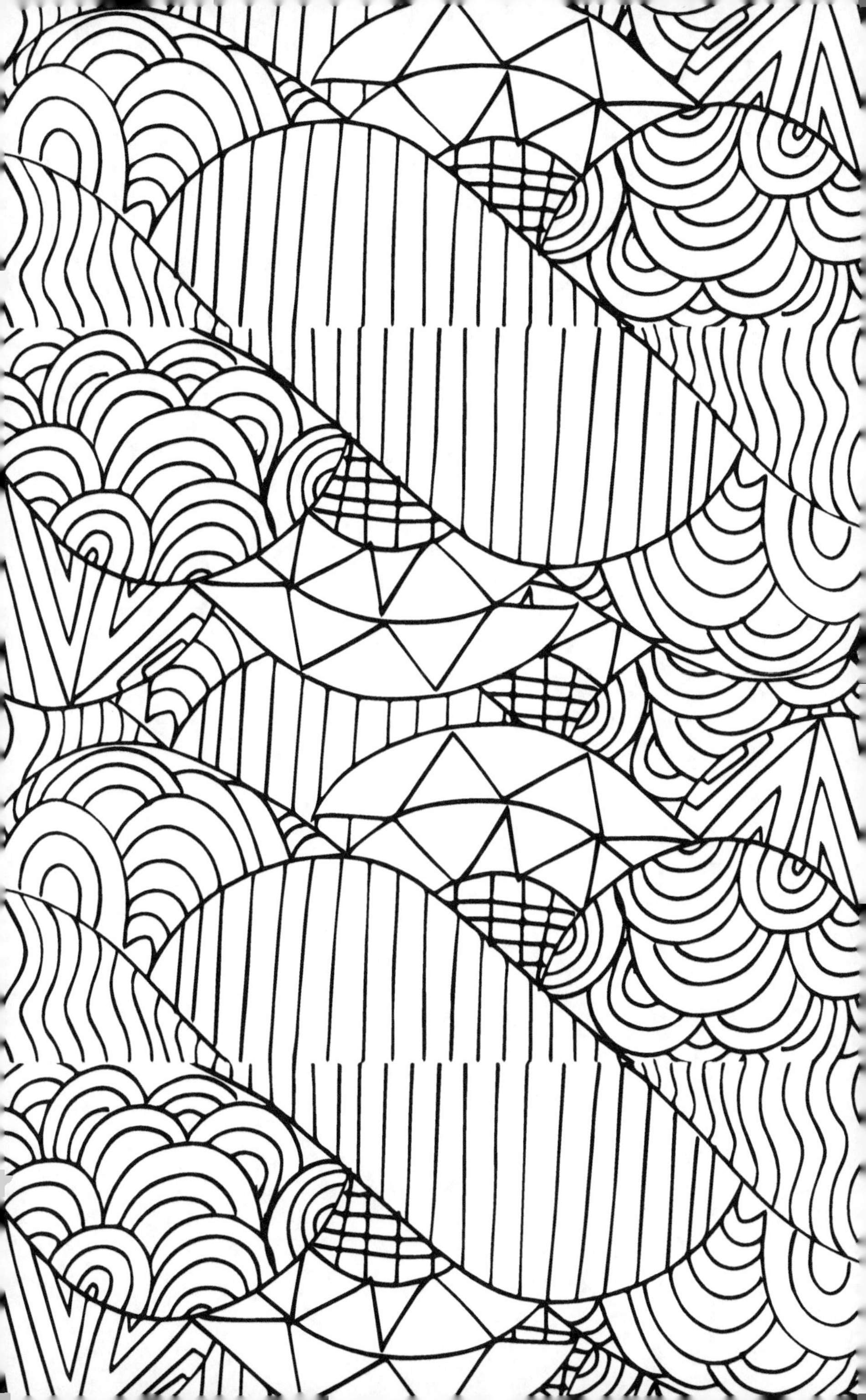

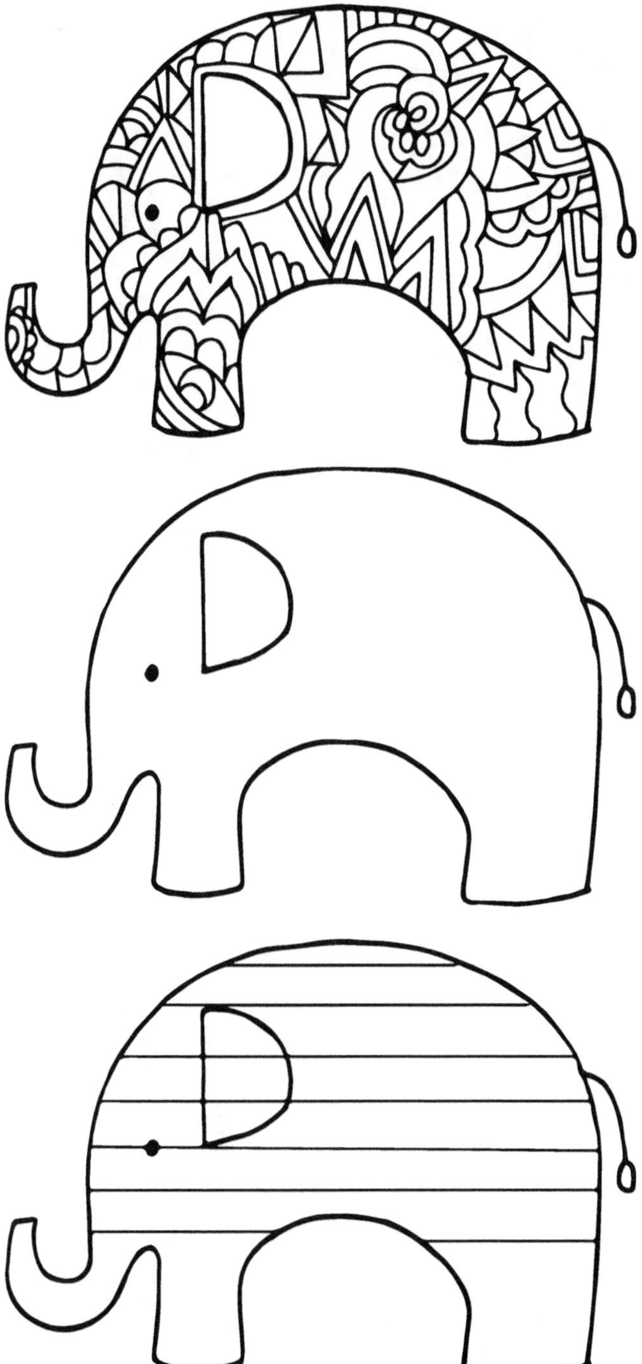

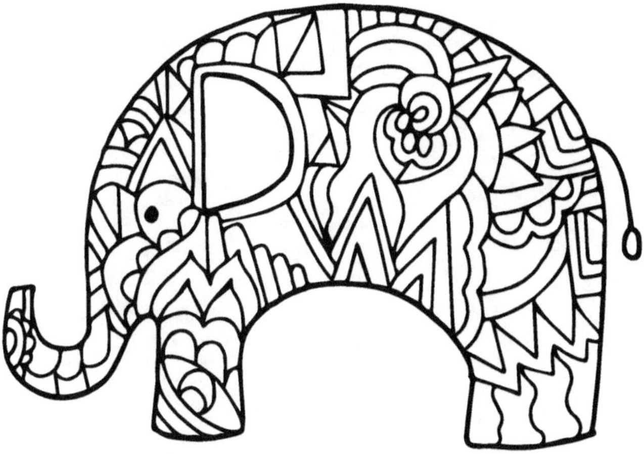

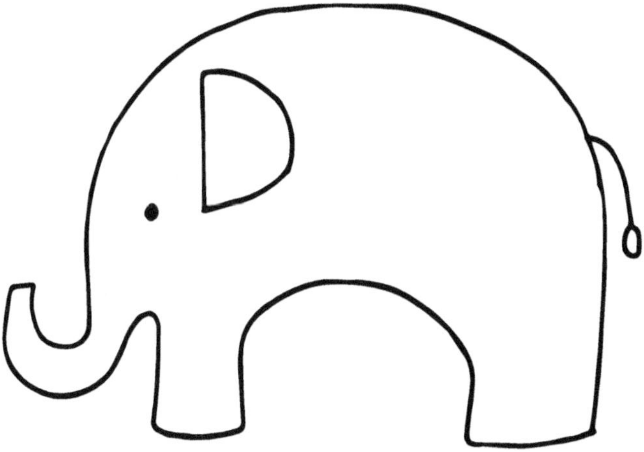

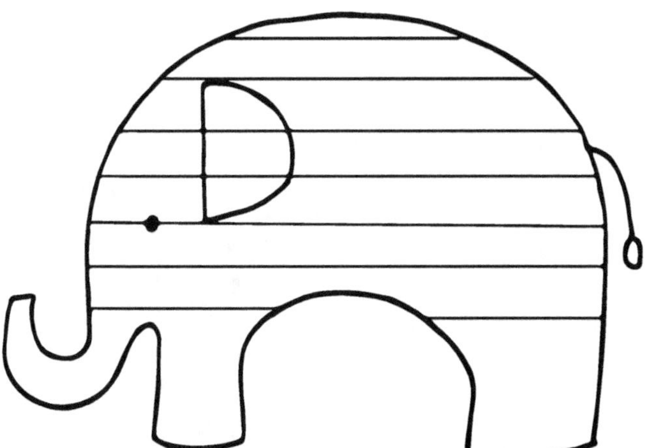

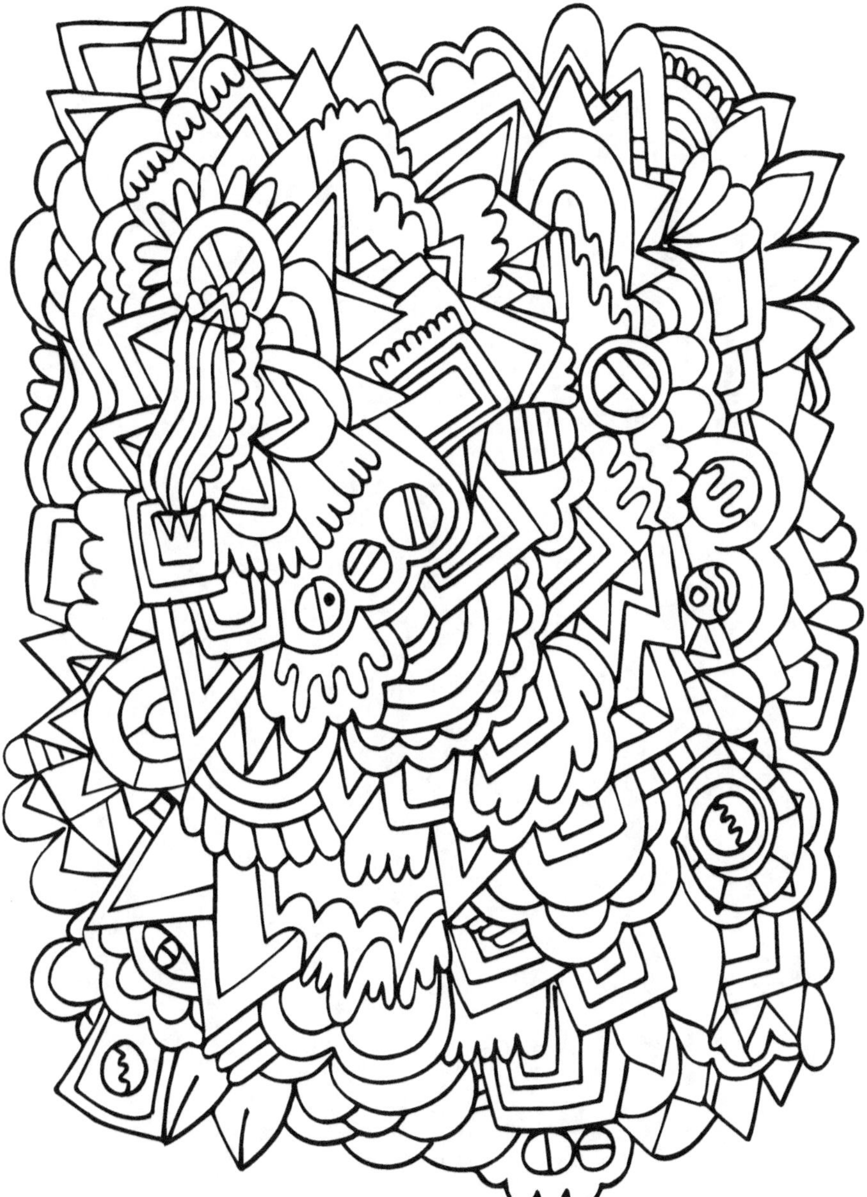

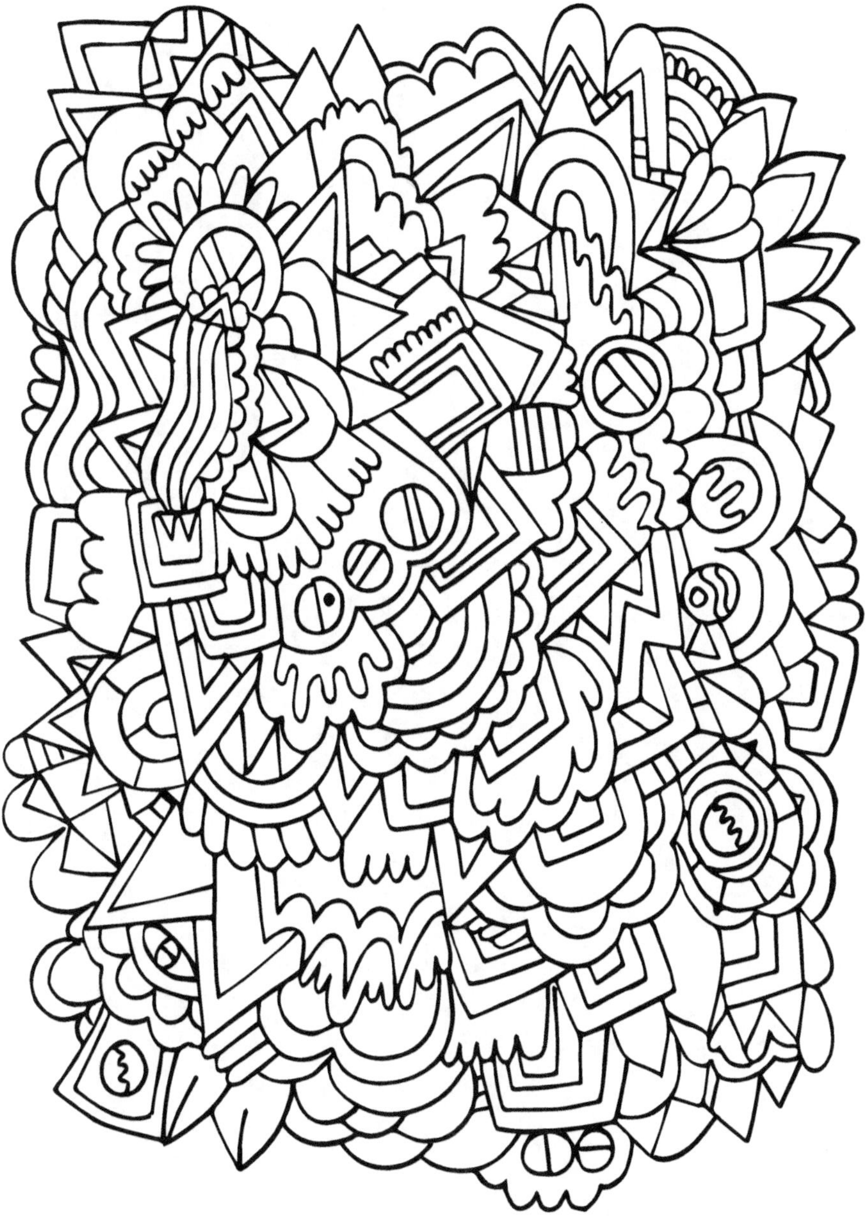

TRUST
THE
PROCESS
OF
LIFE

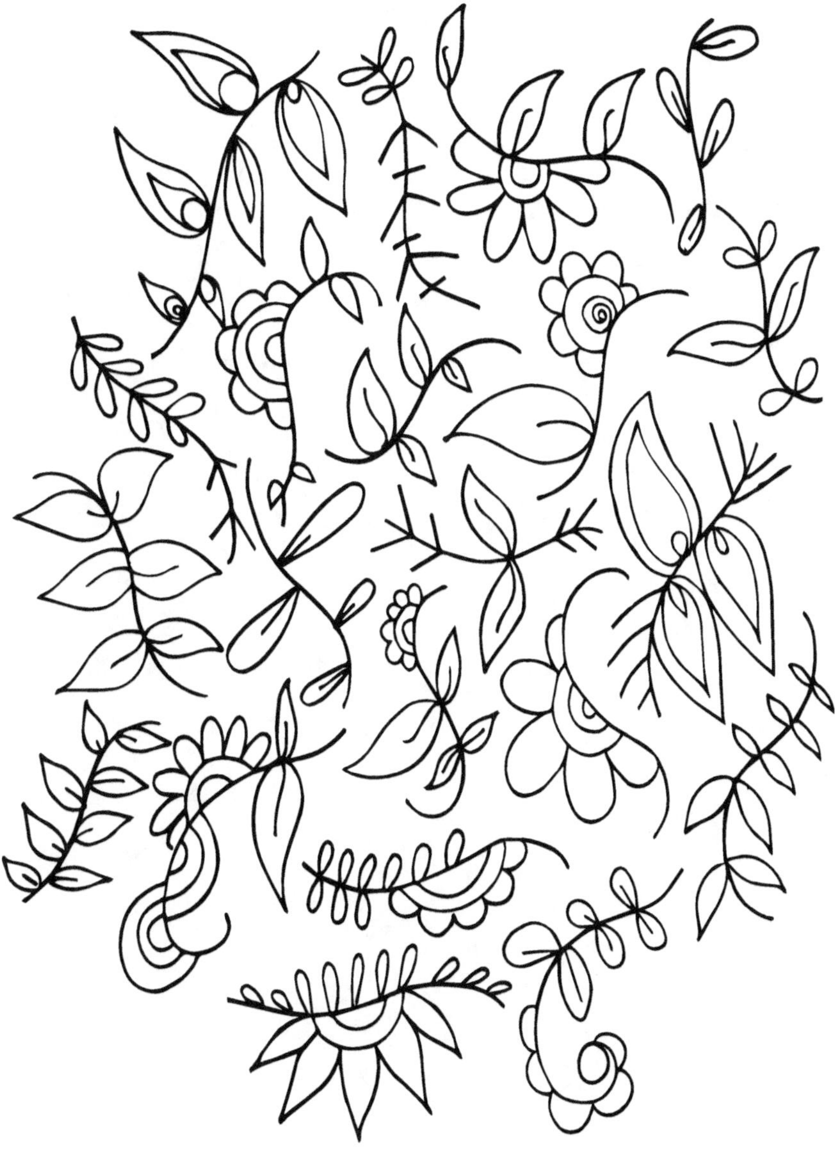

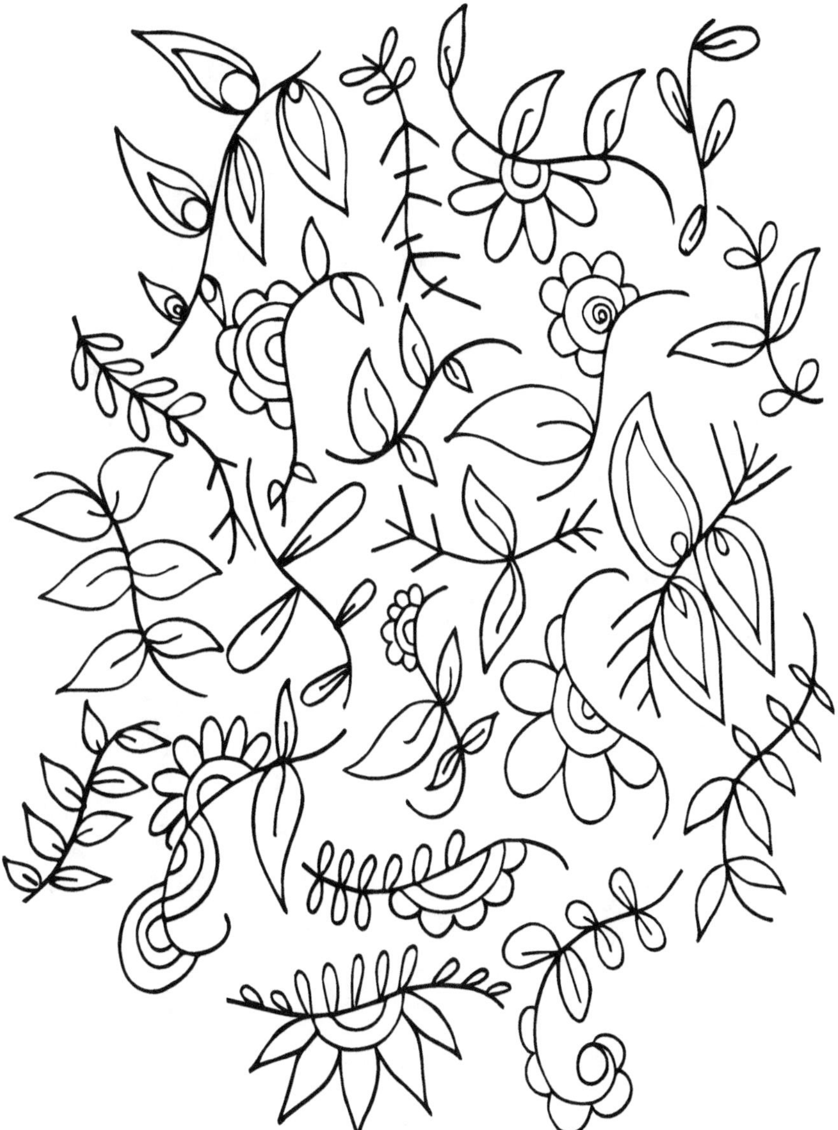

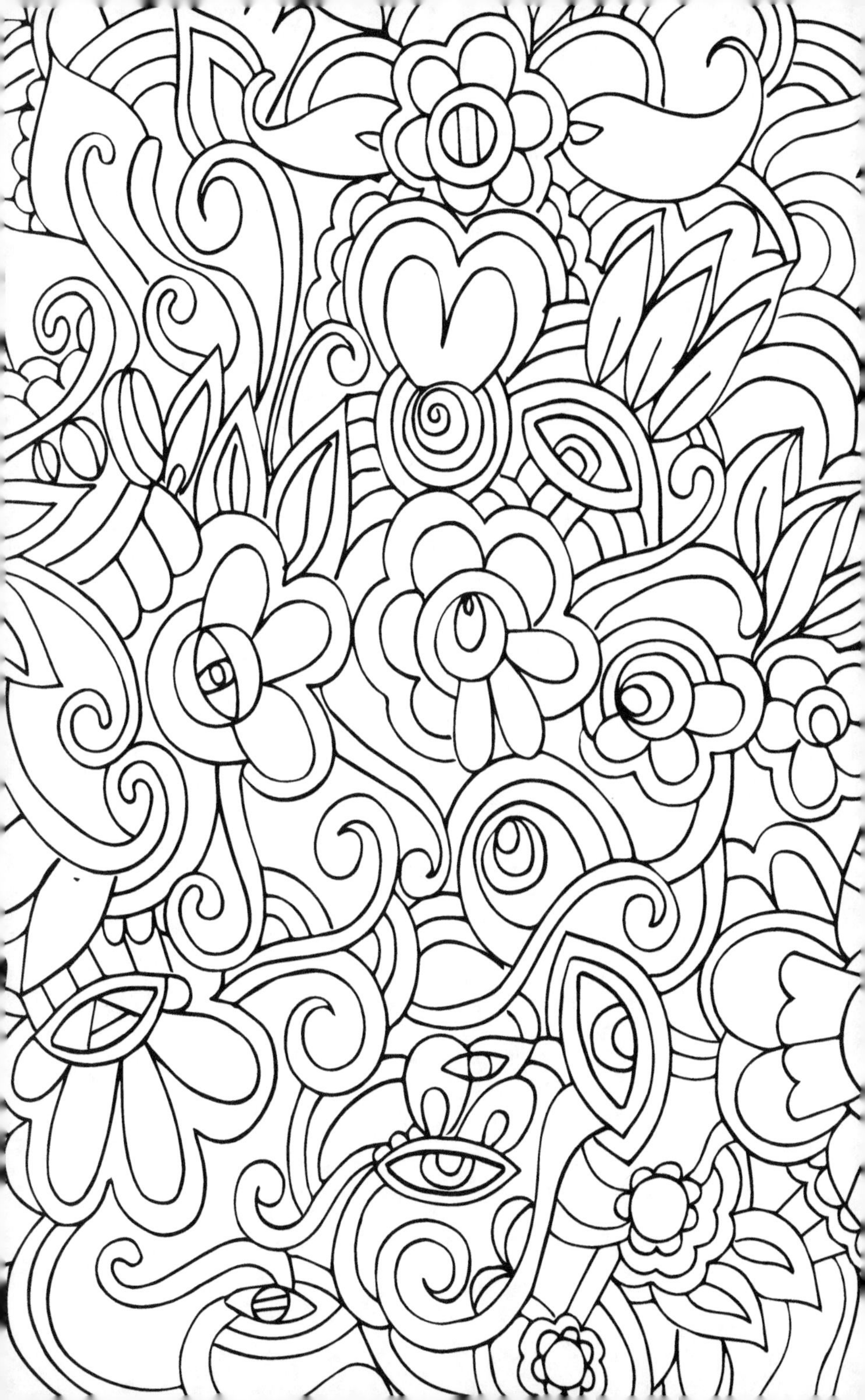

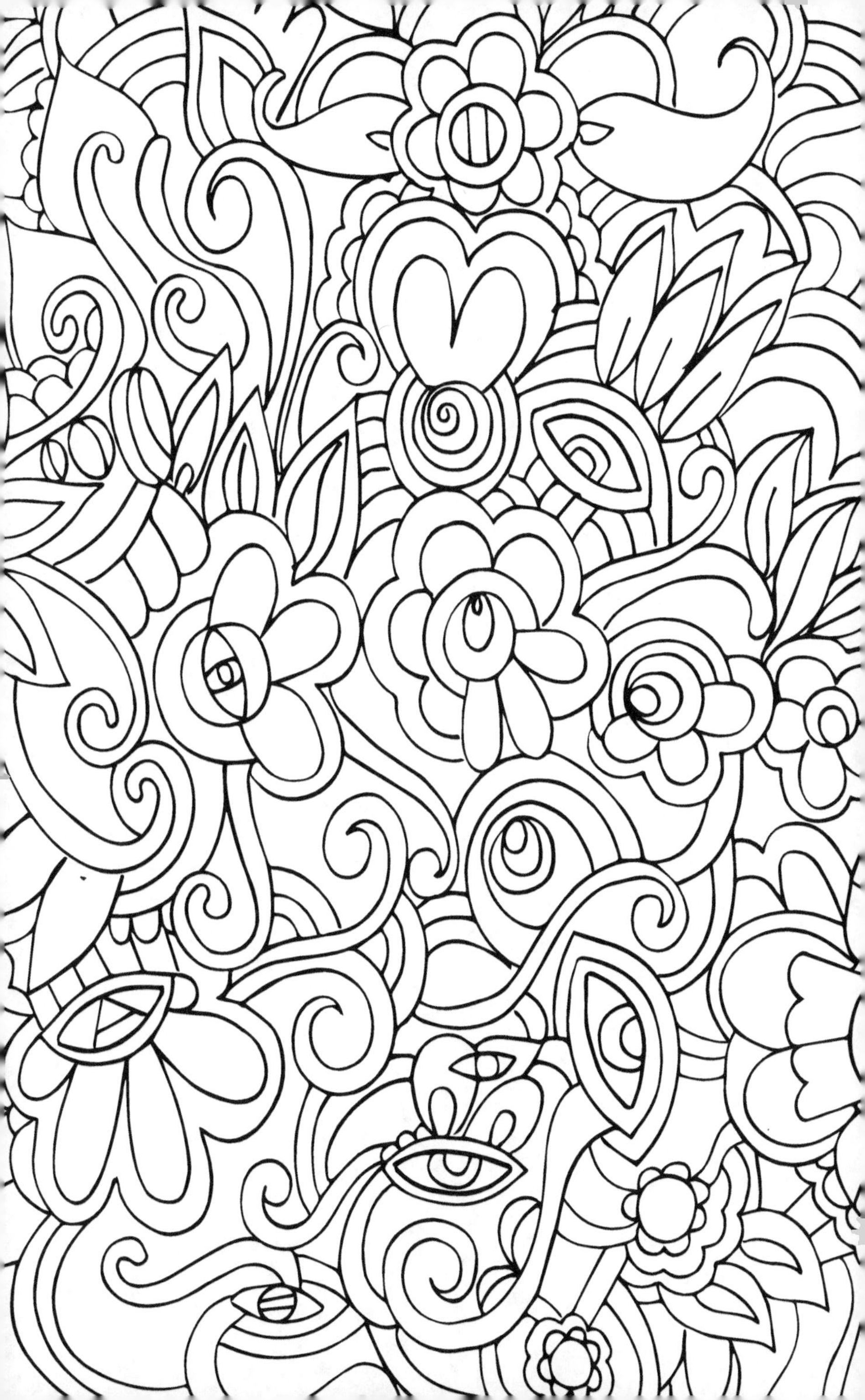

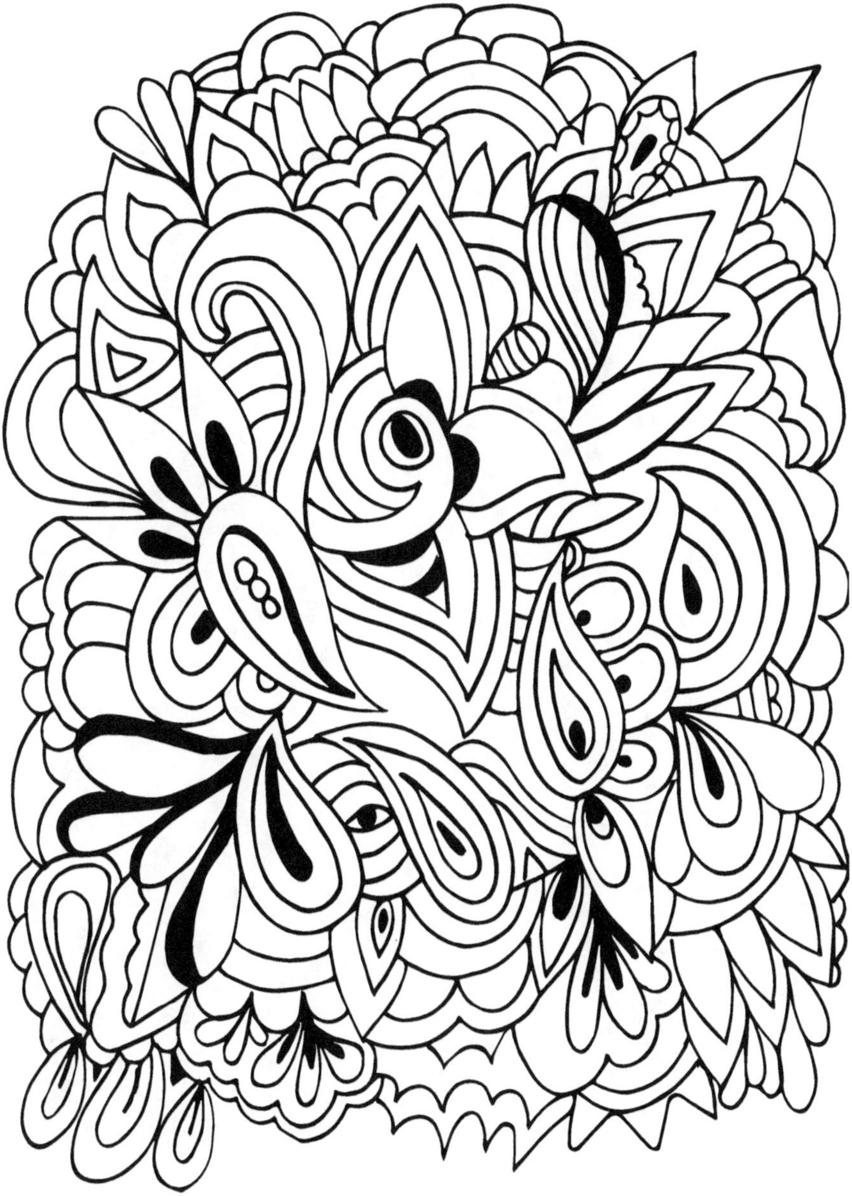

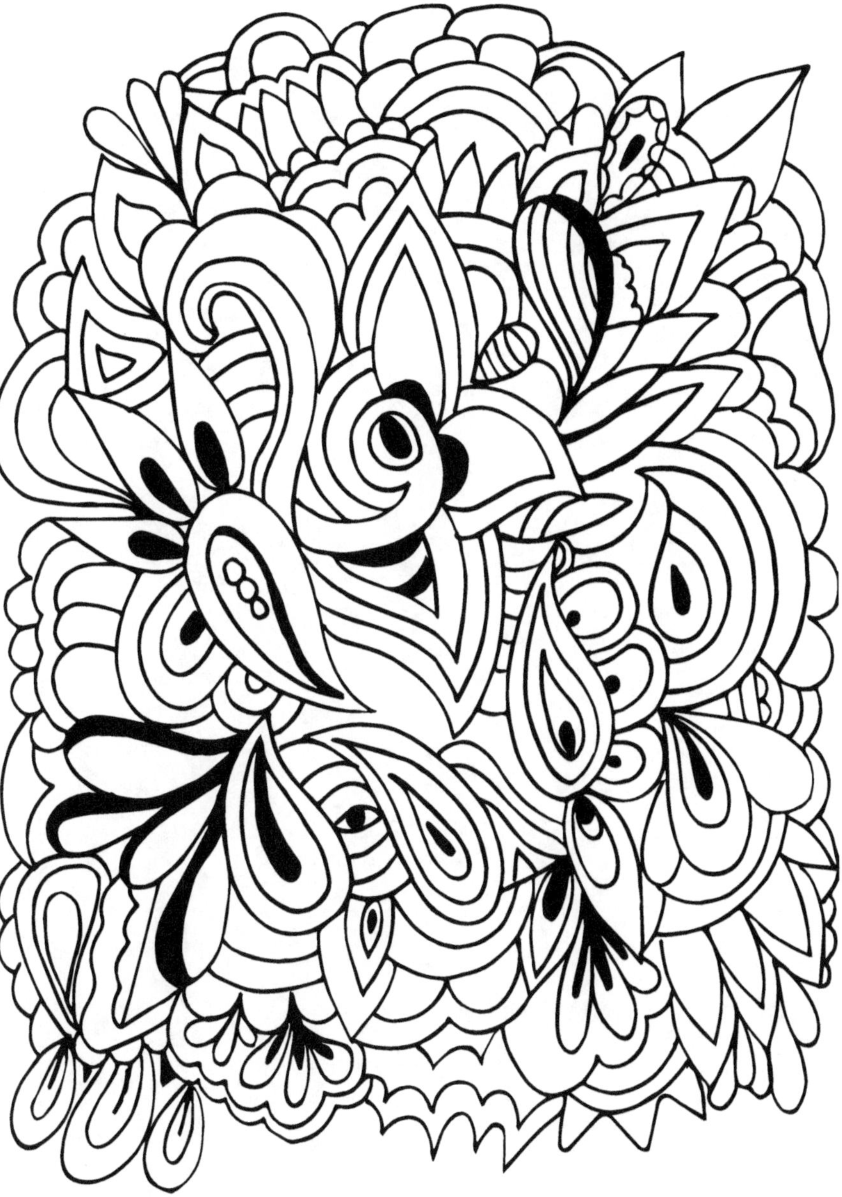

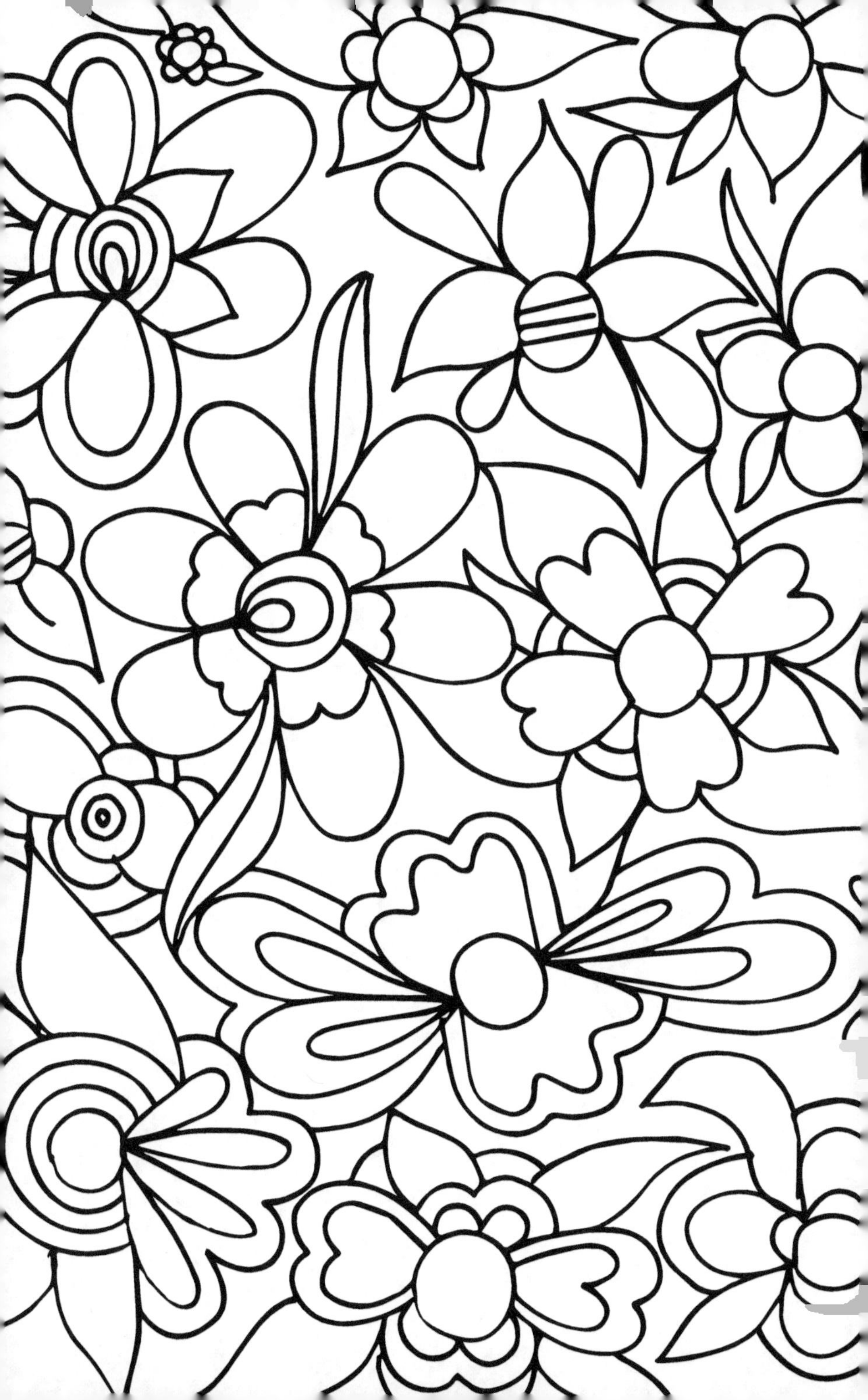

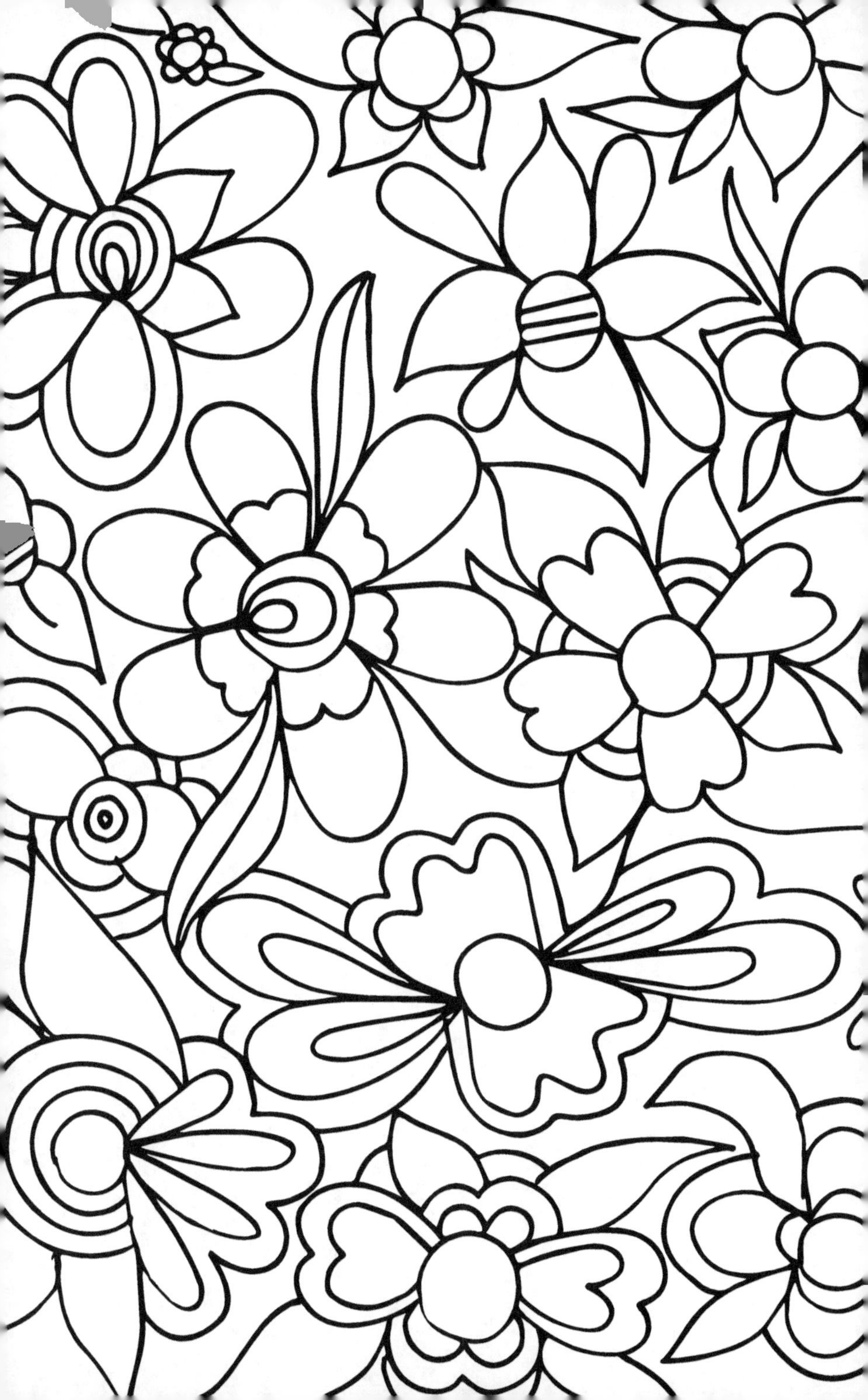

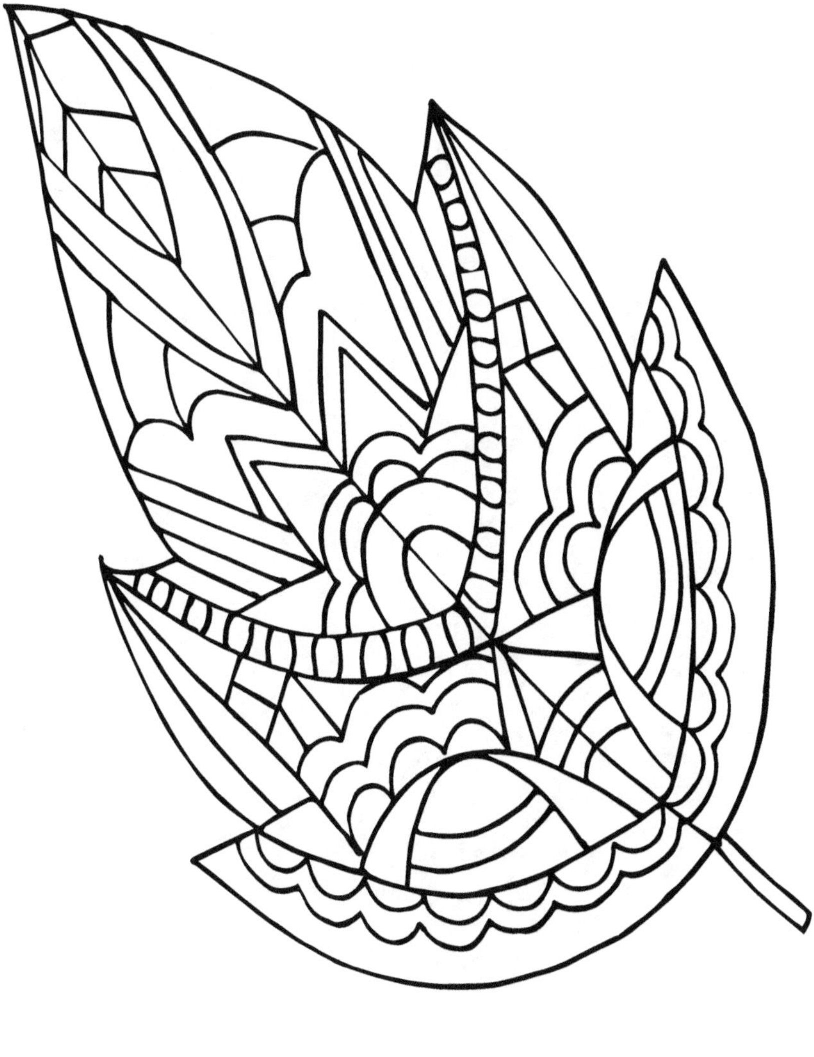

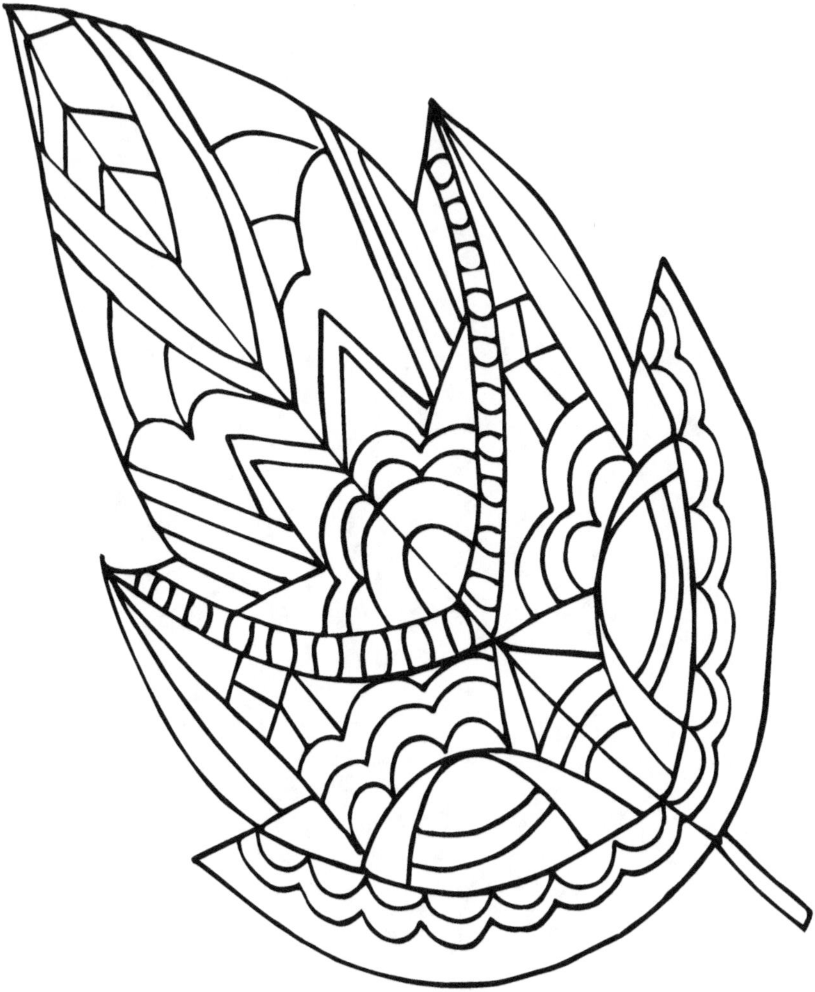

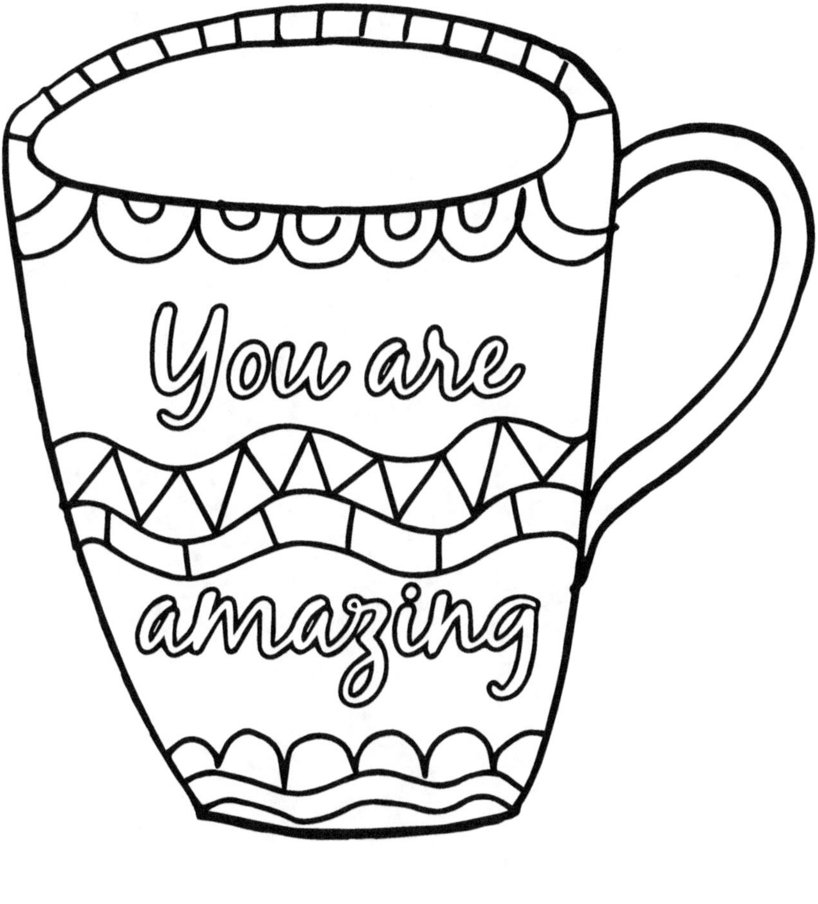
You are
amazing

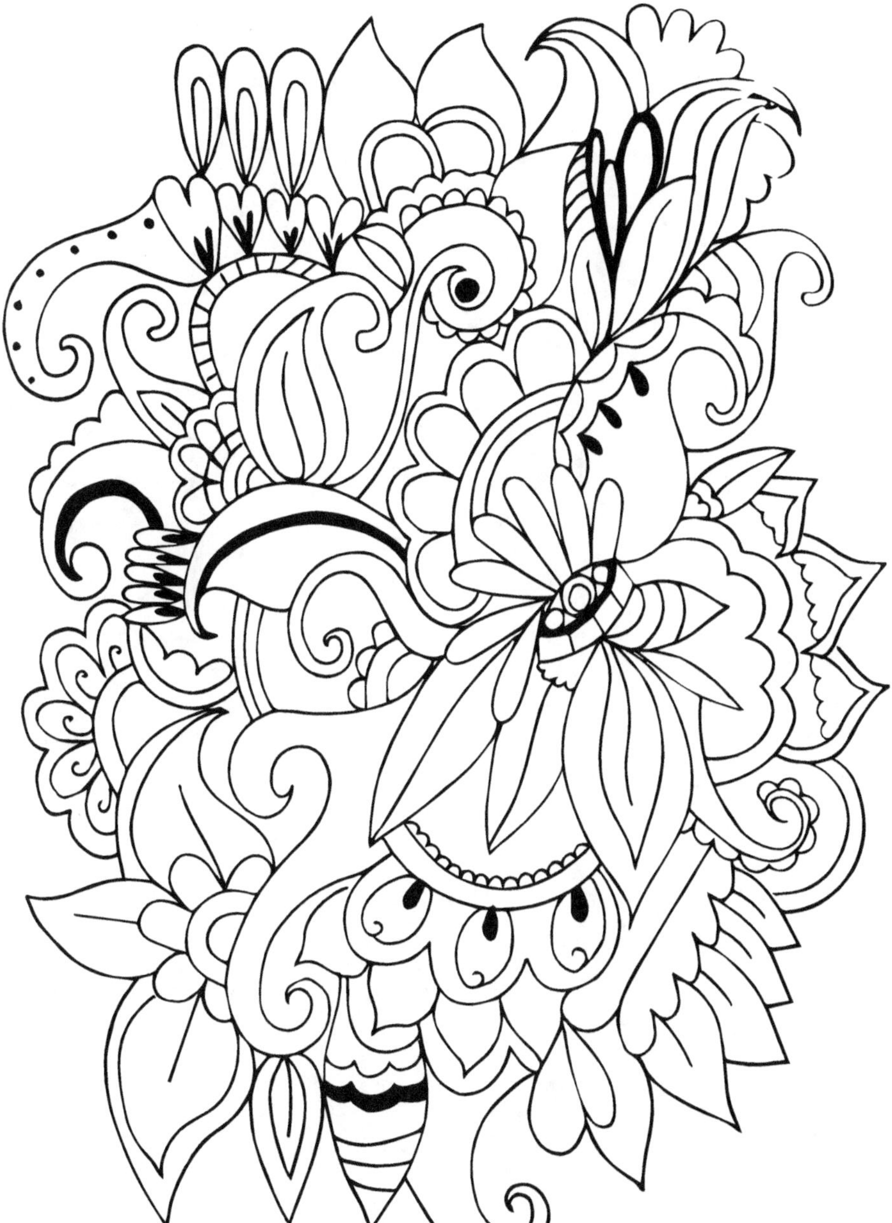

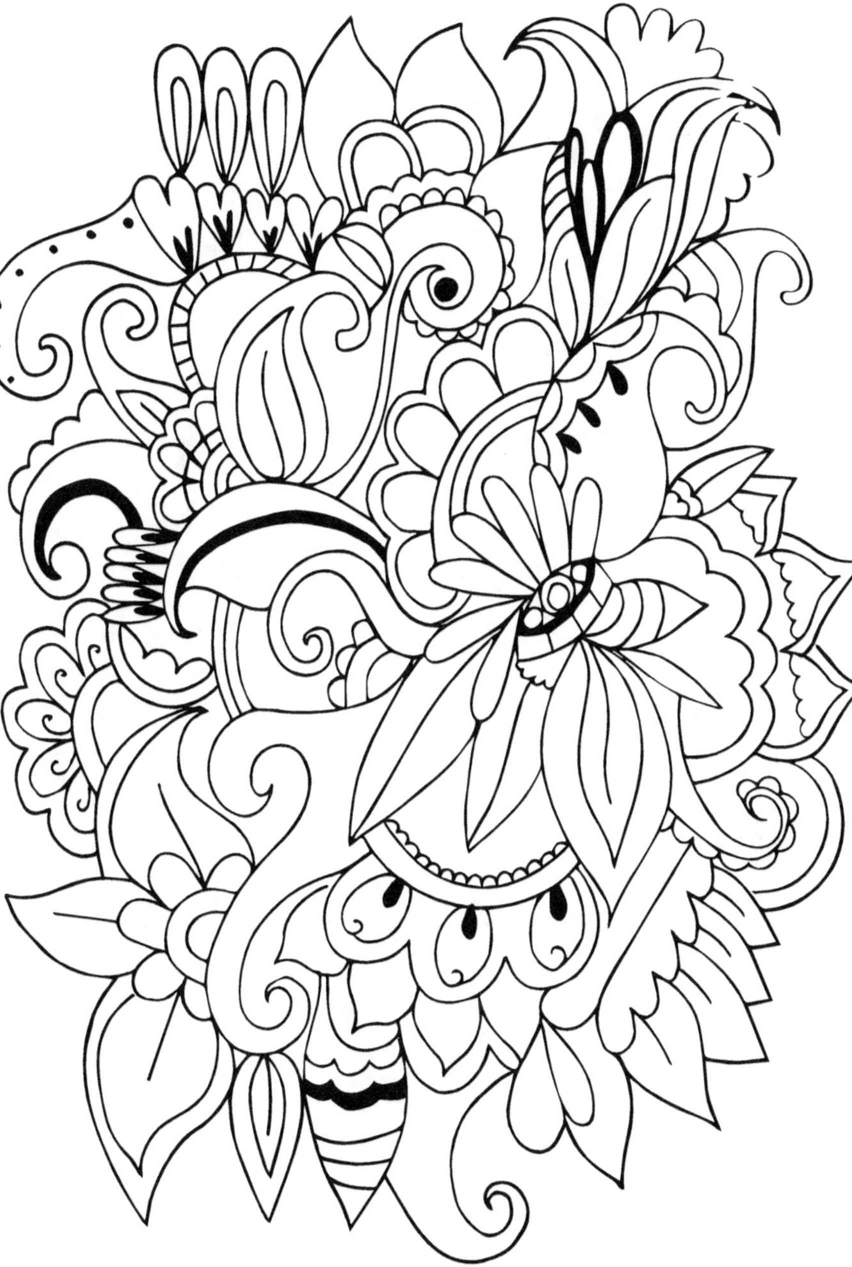

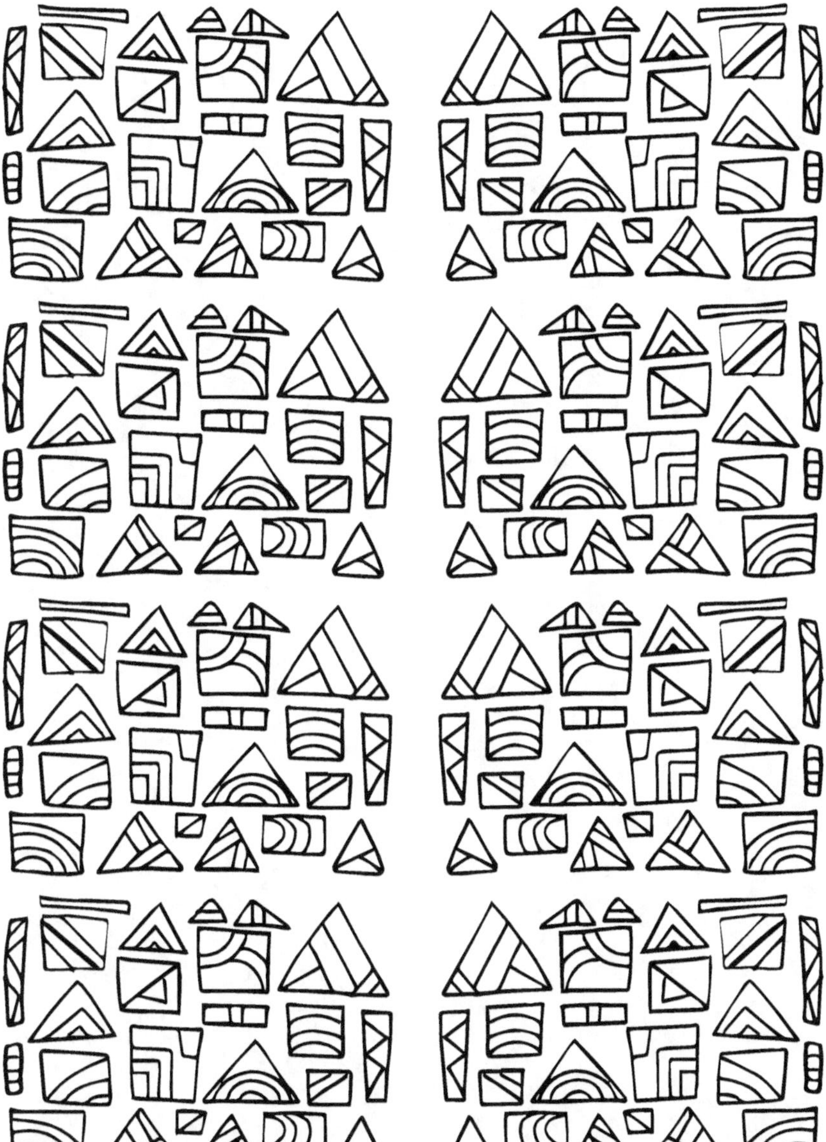

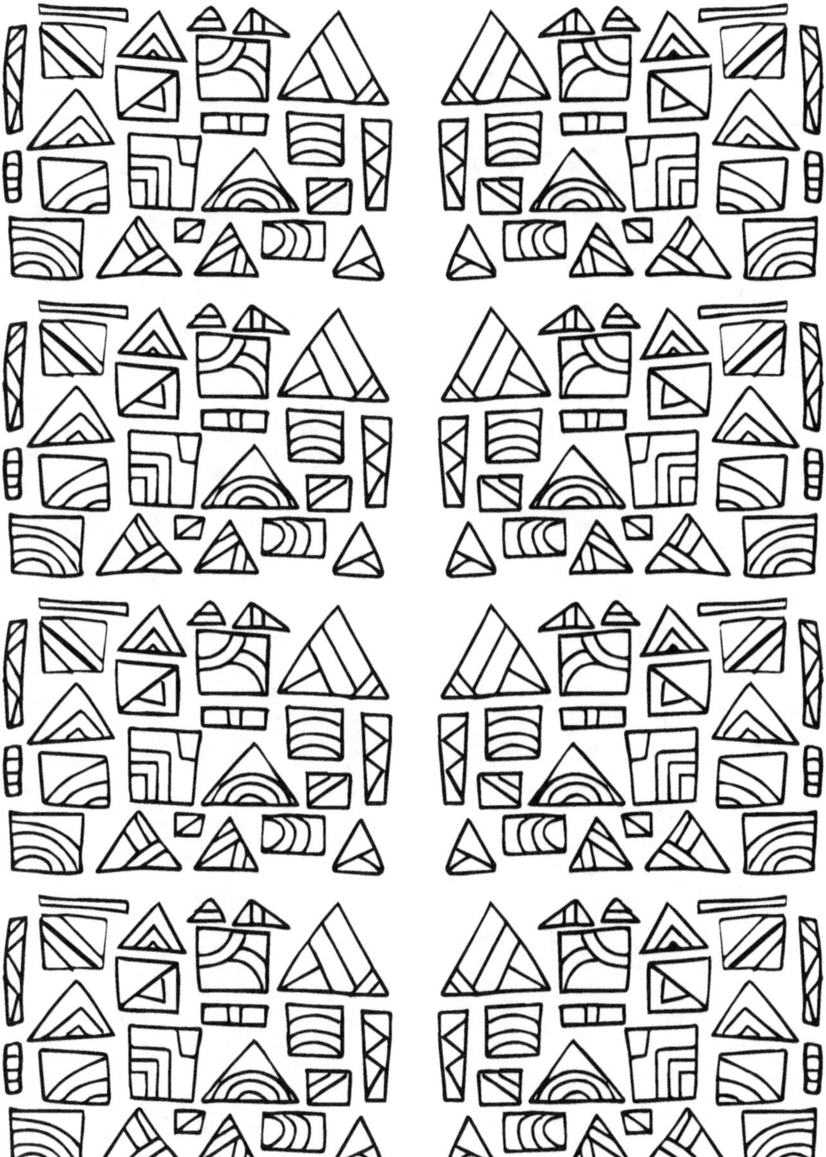

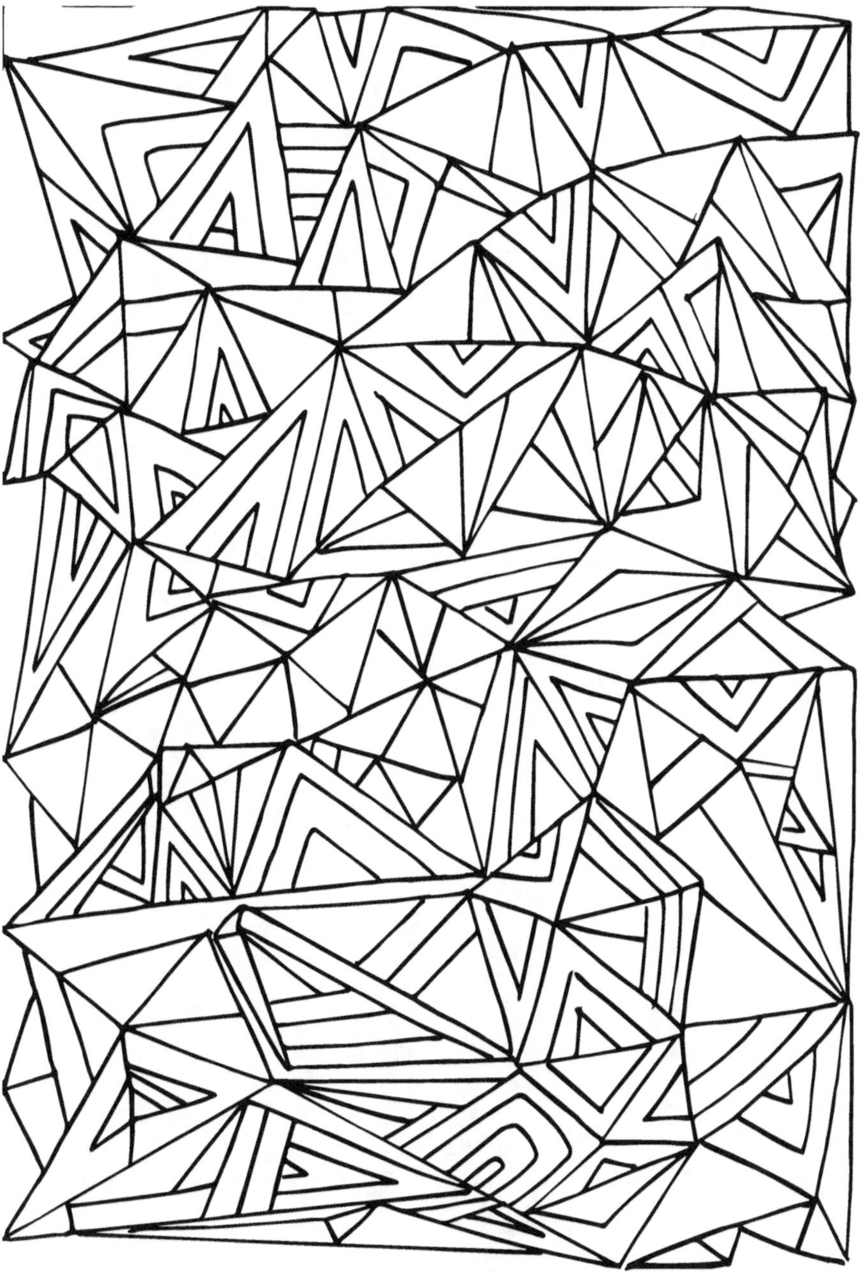

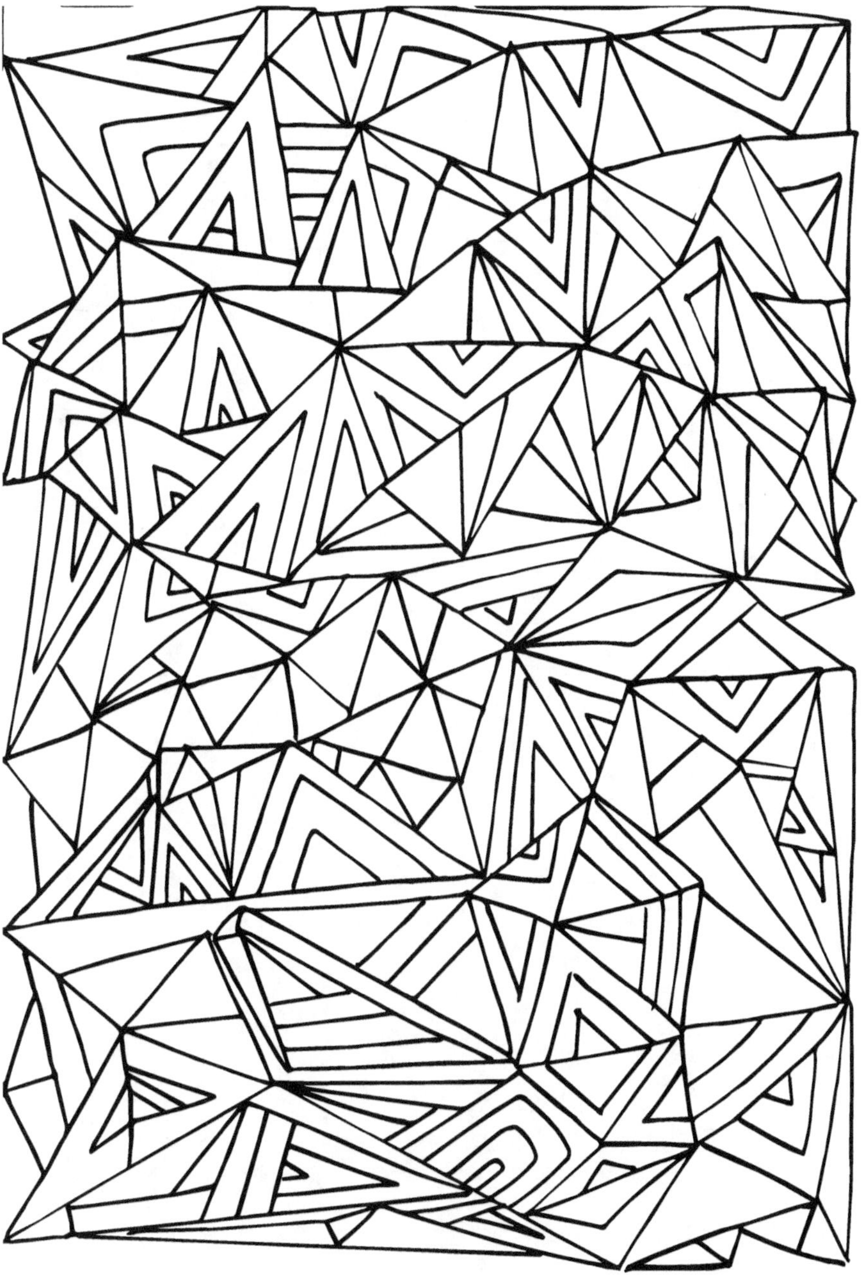

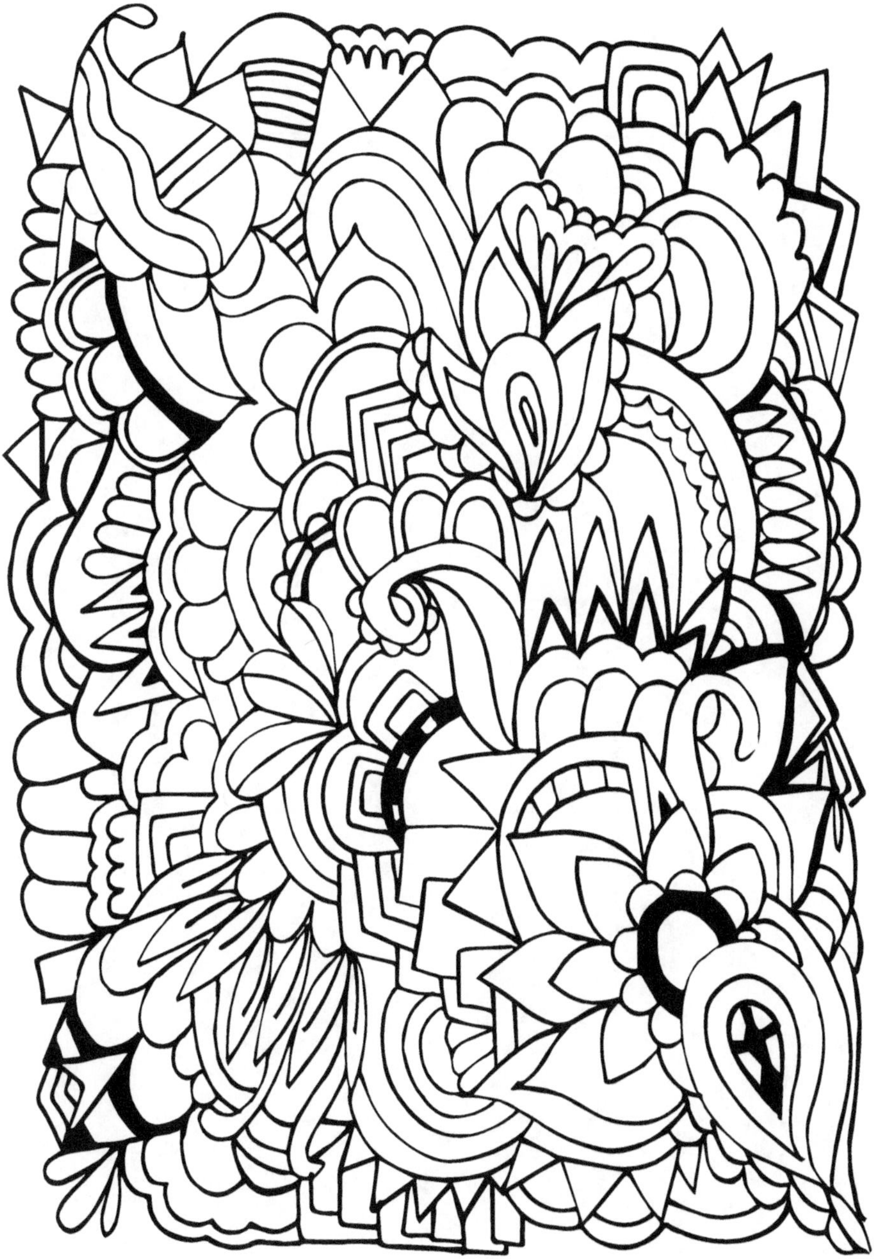

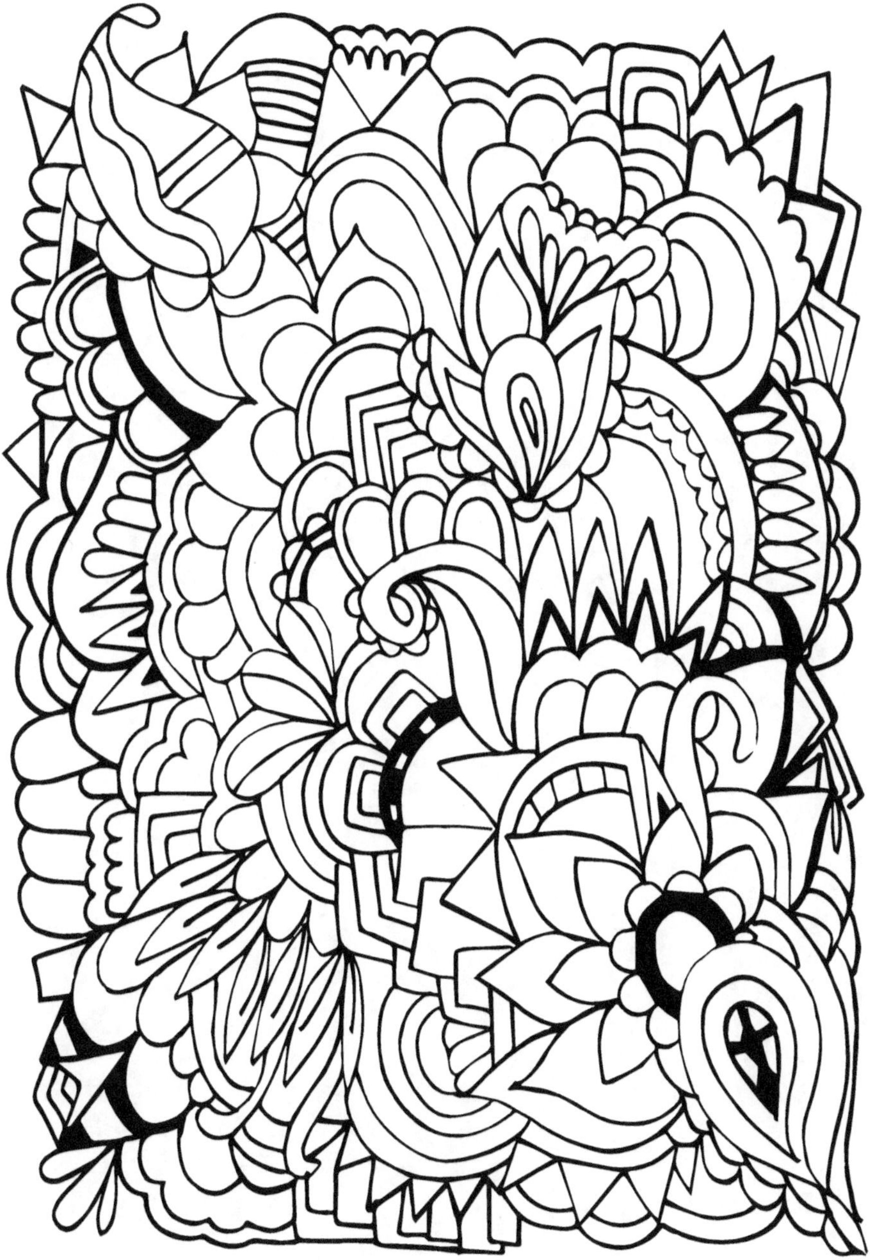

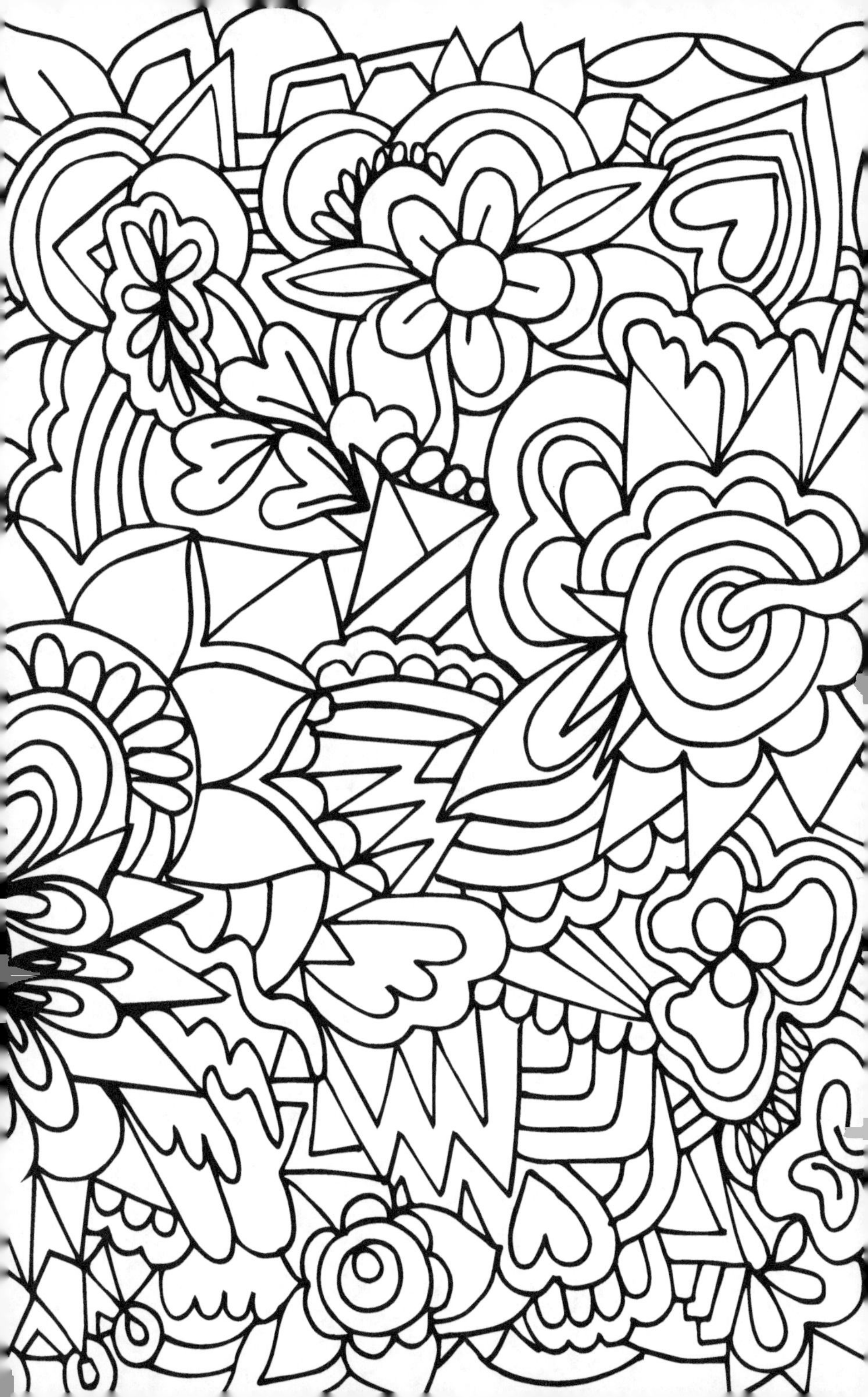

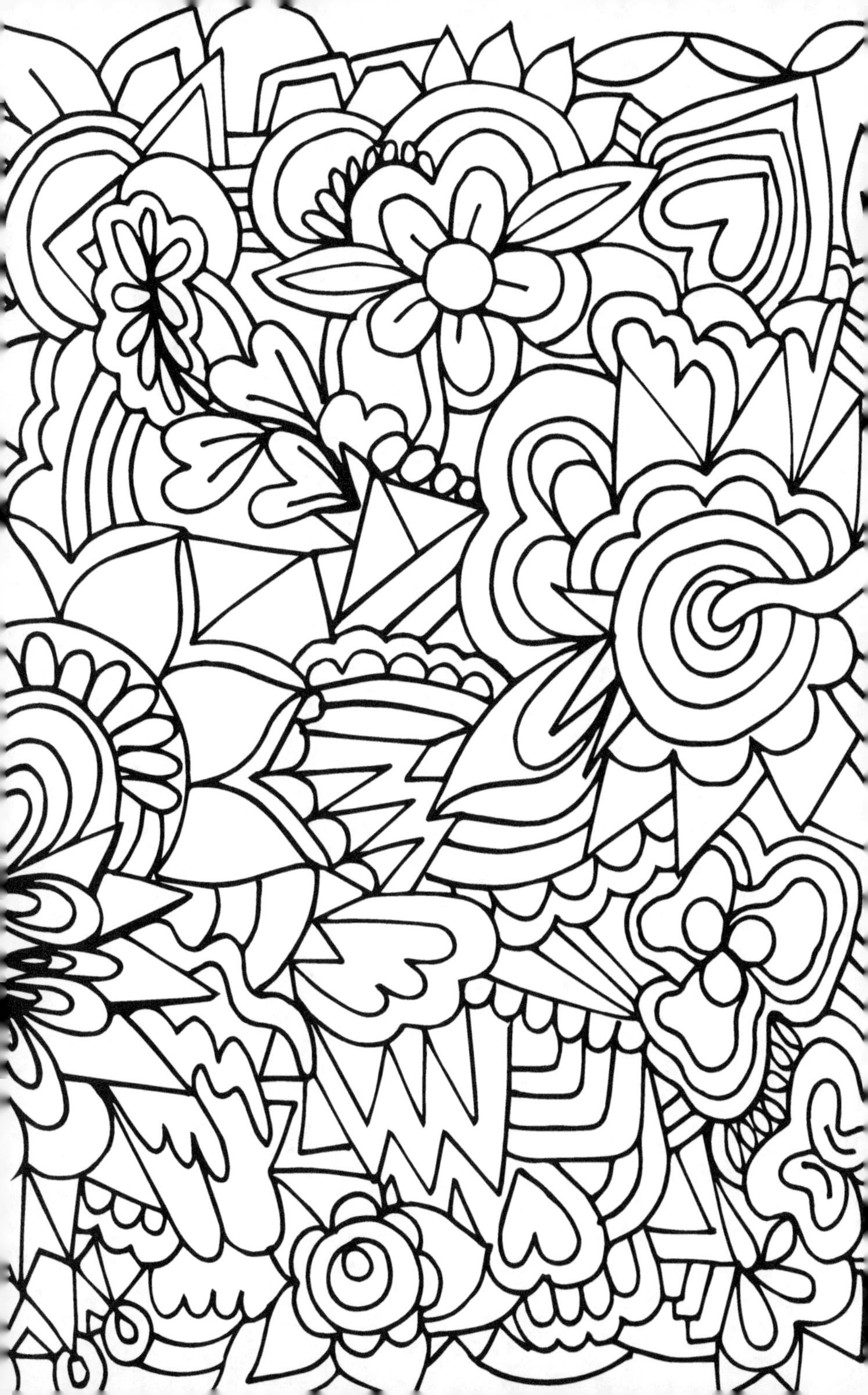

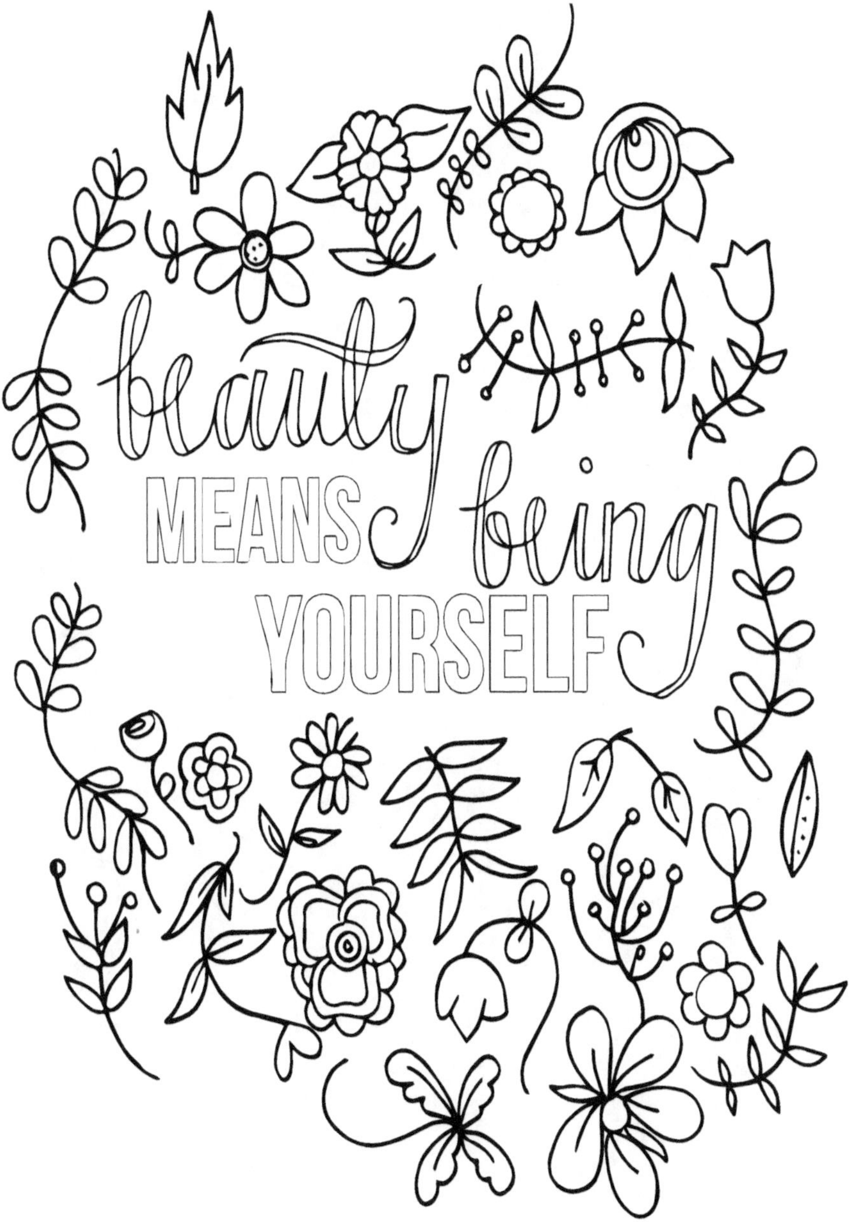
beauty
MEANS being
YOURSELF

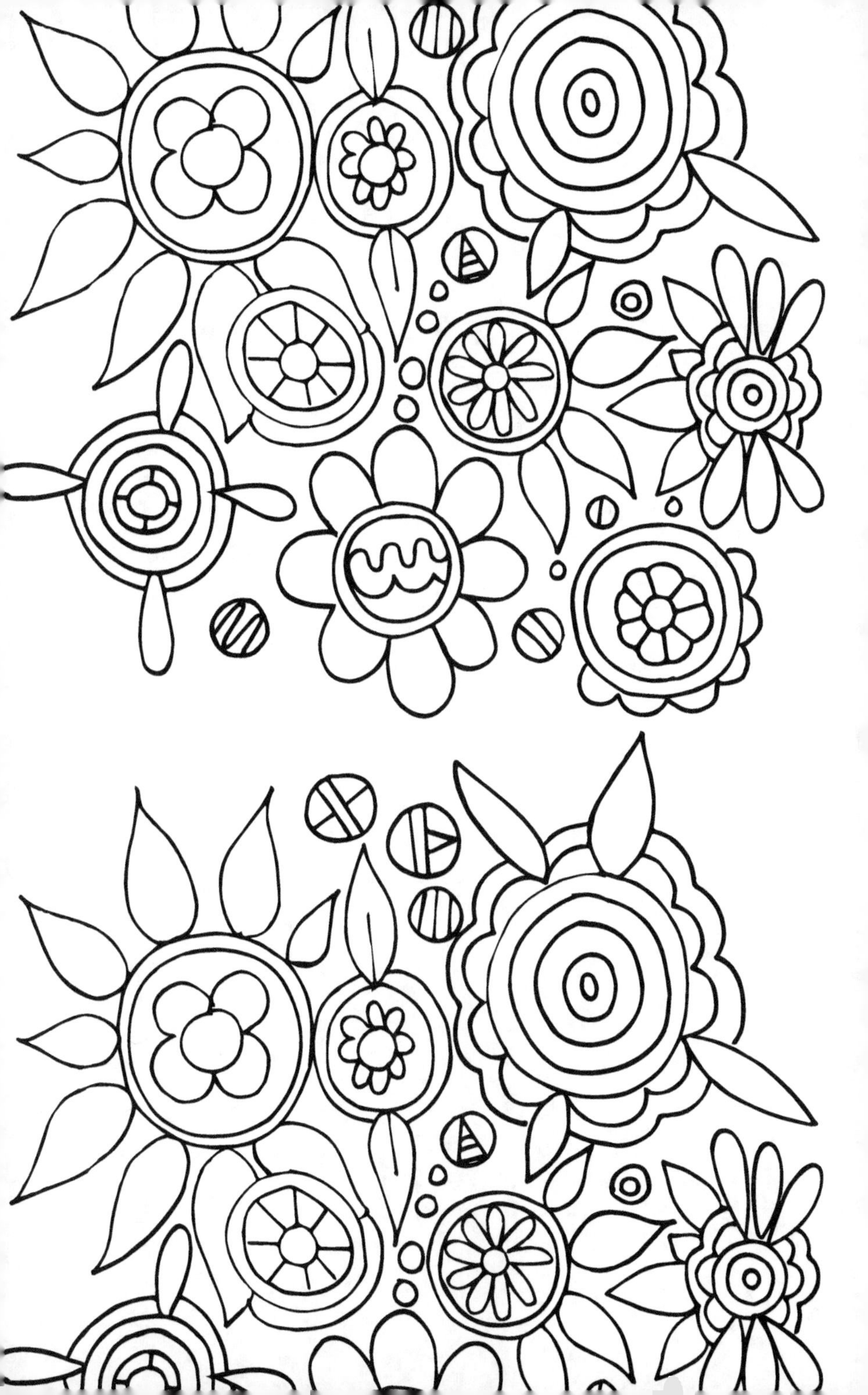

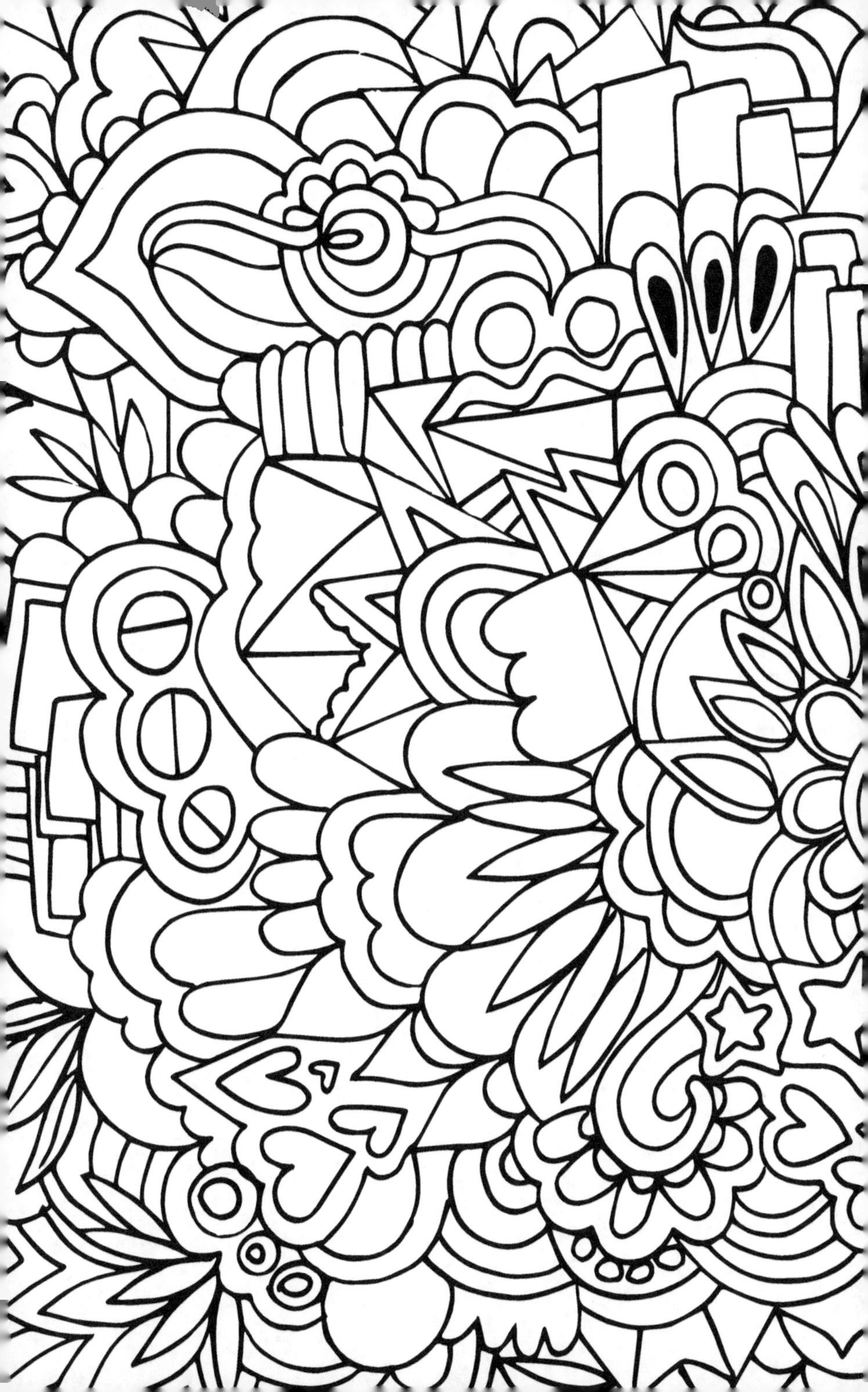

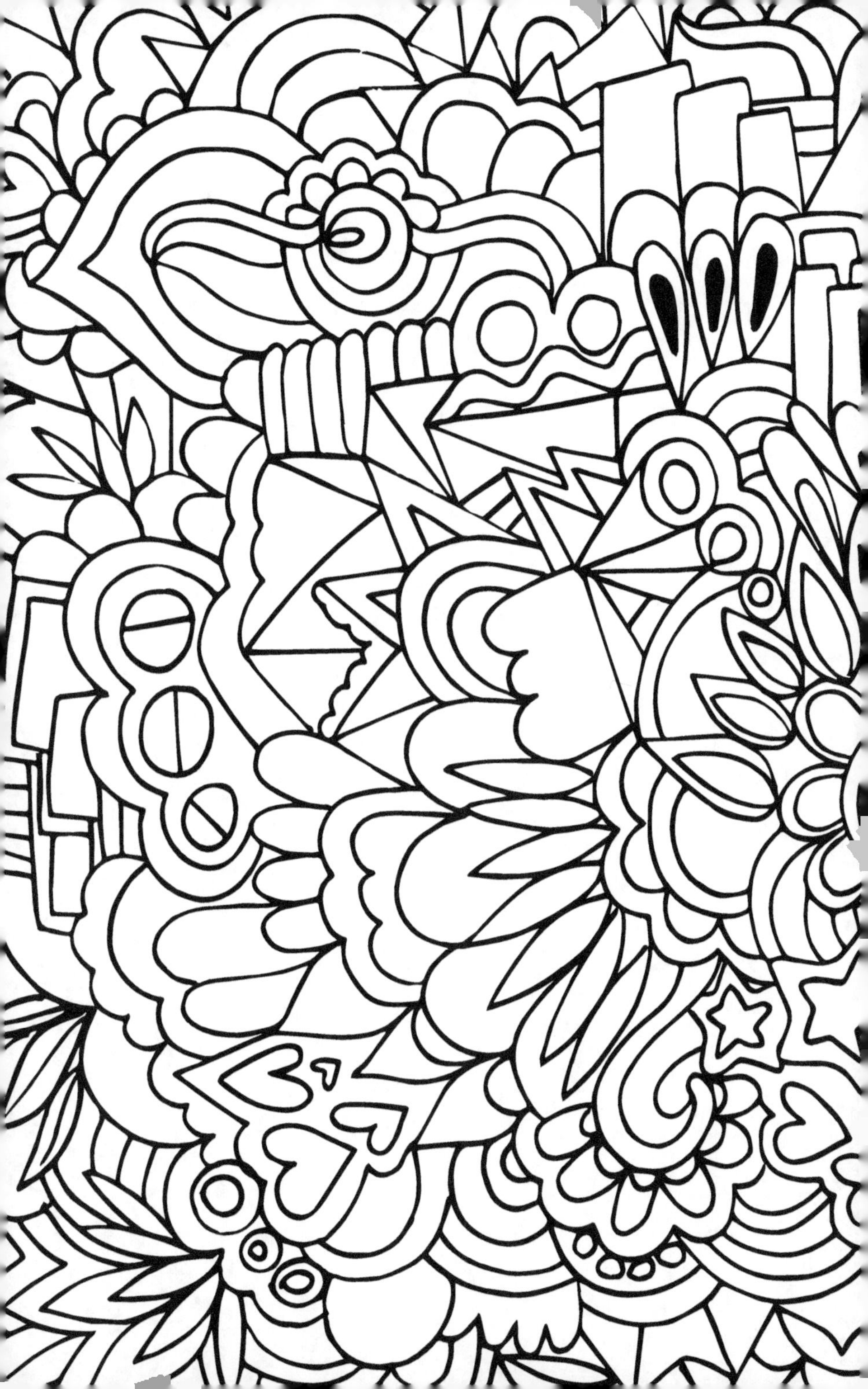

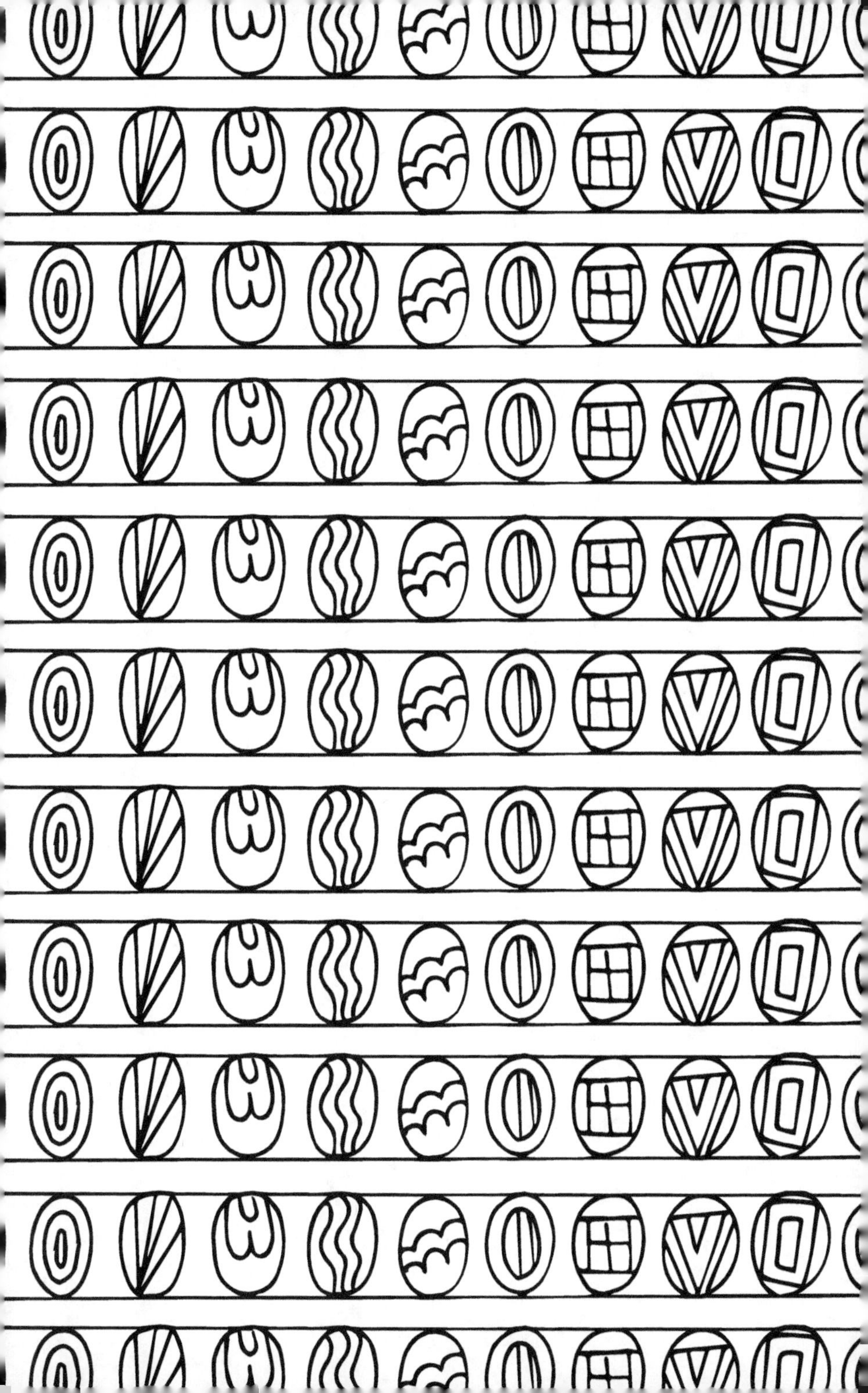

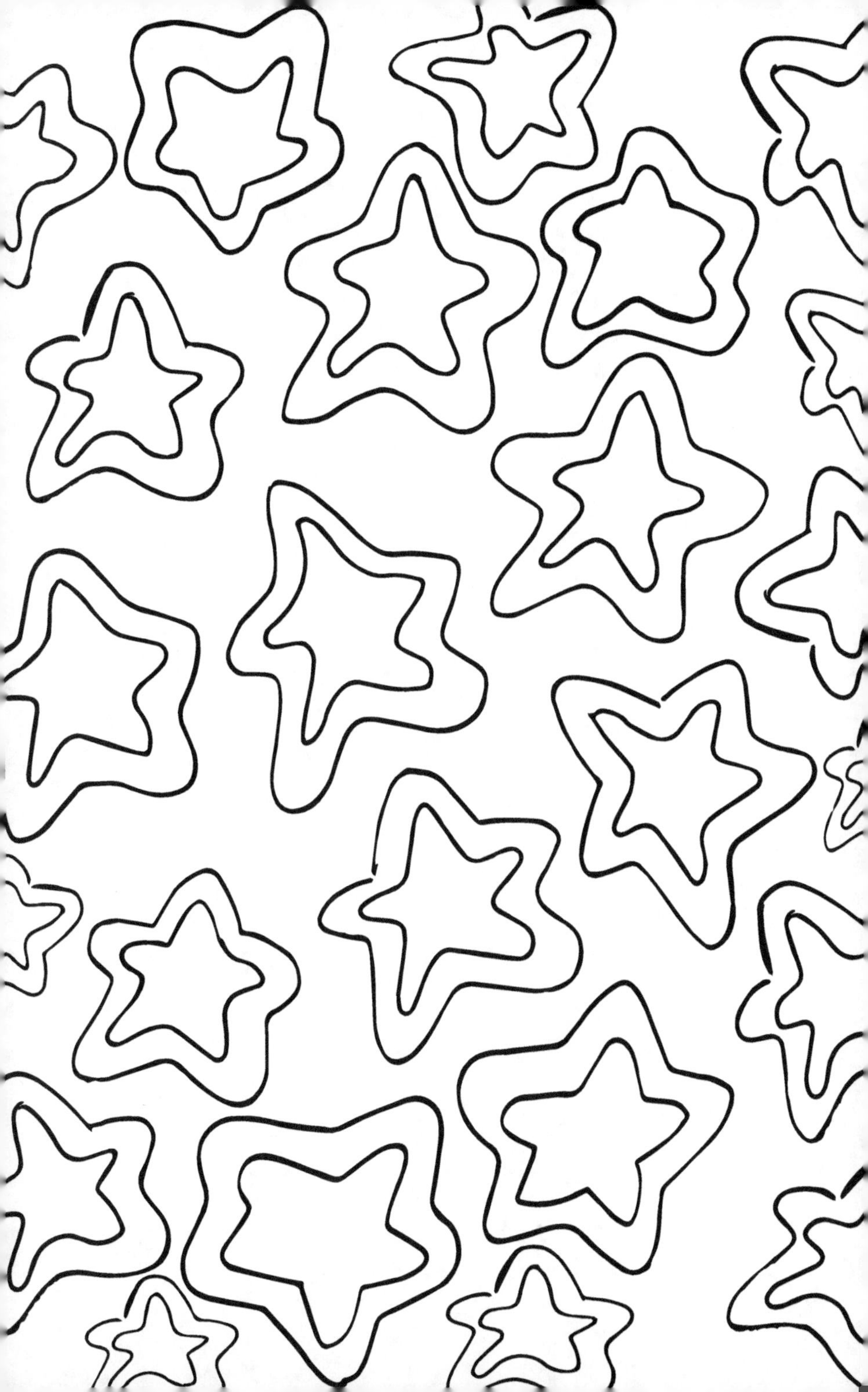

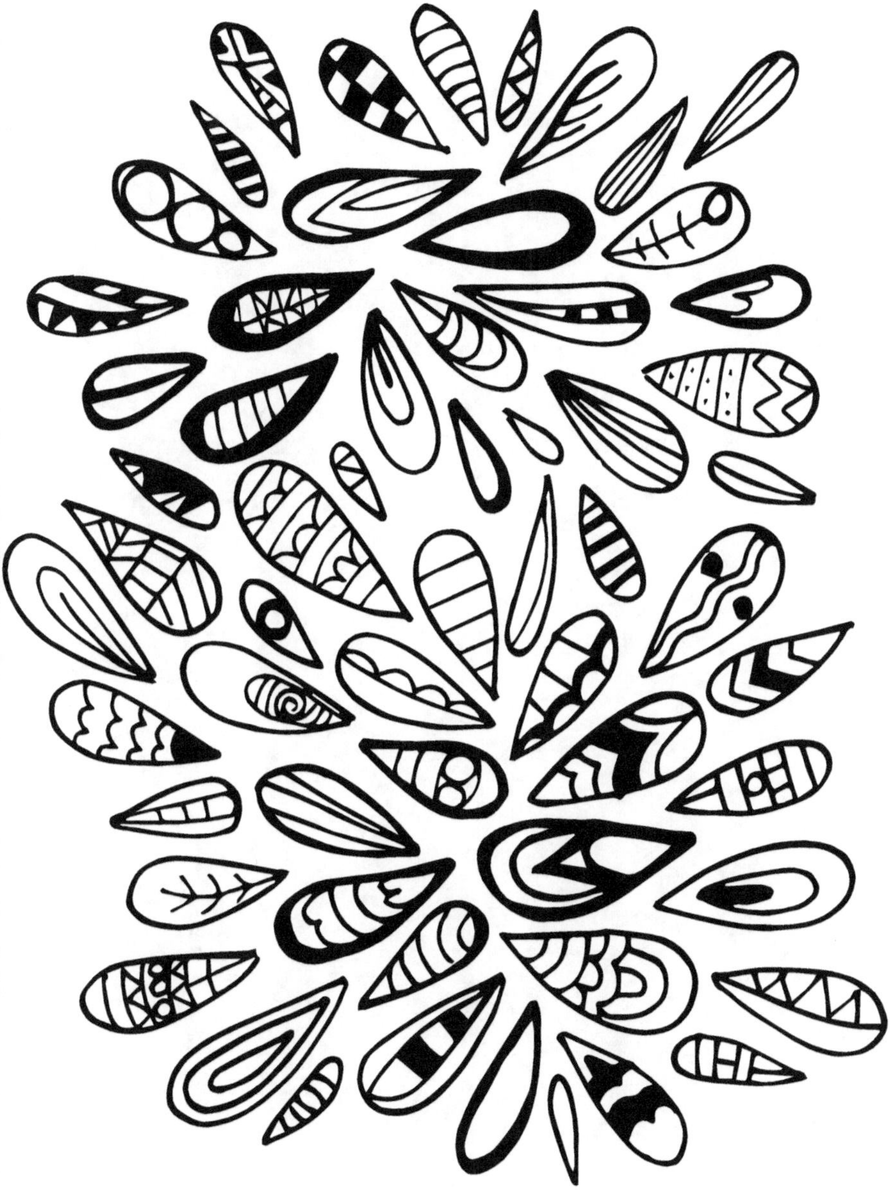

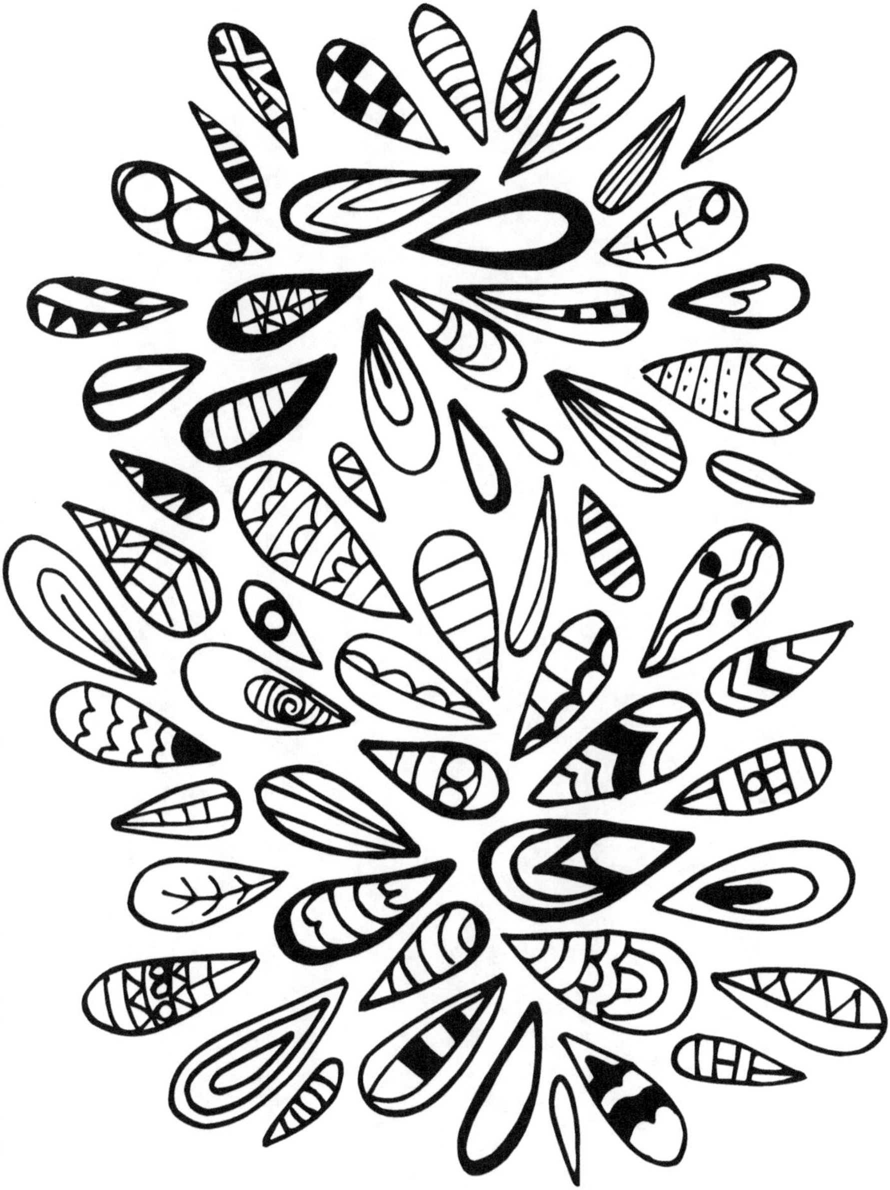

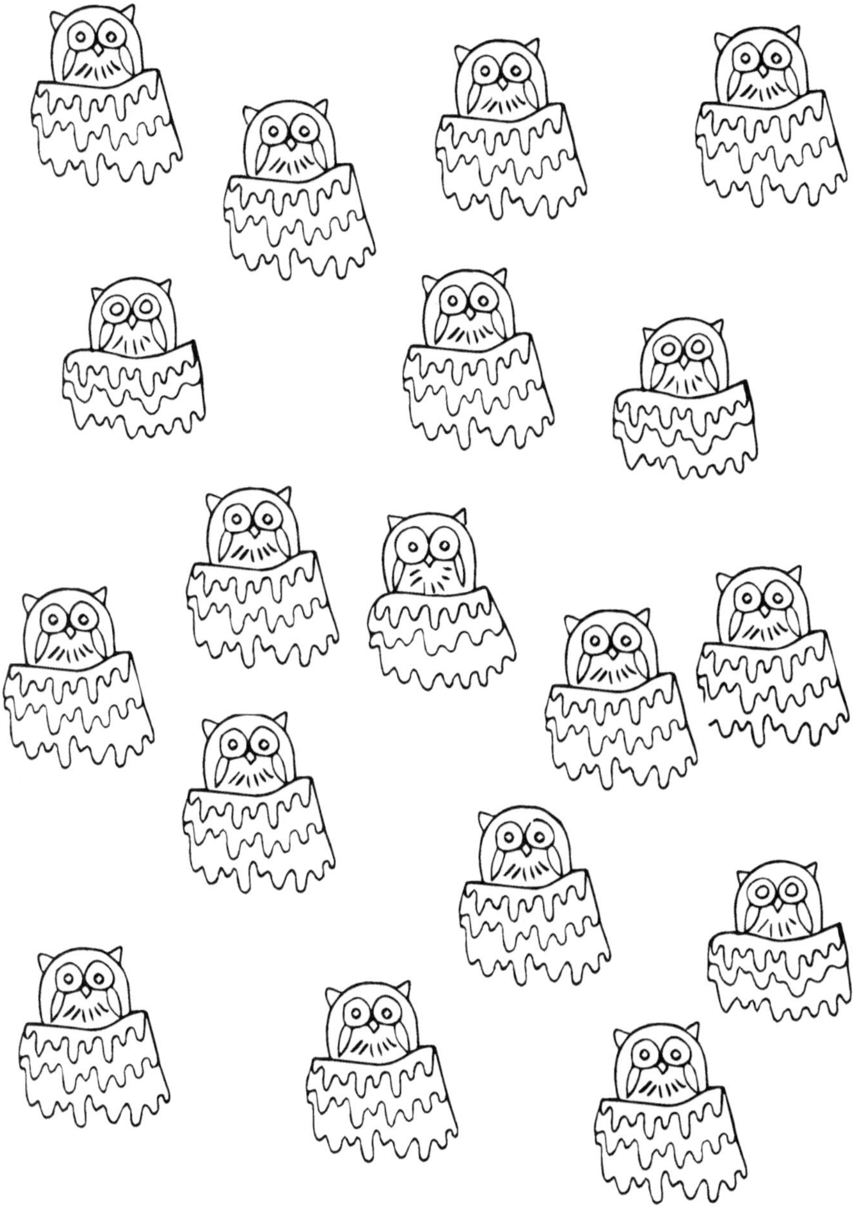

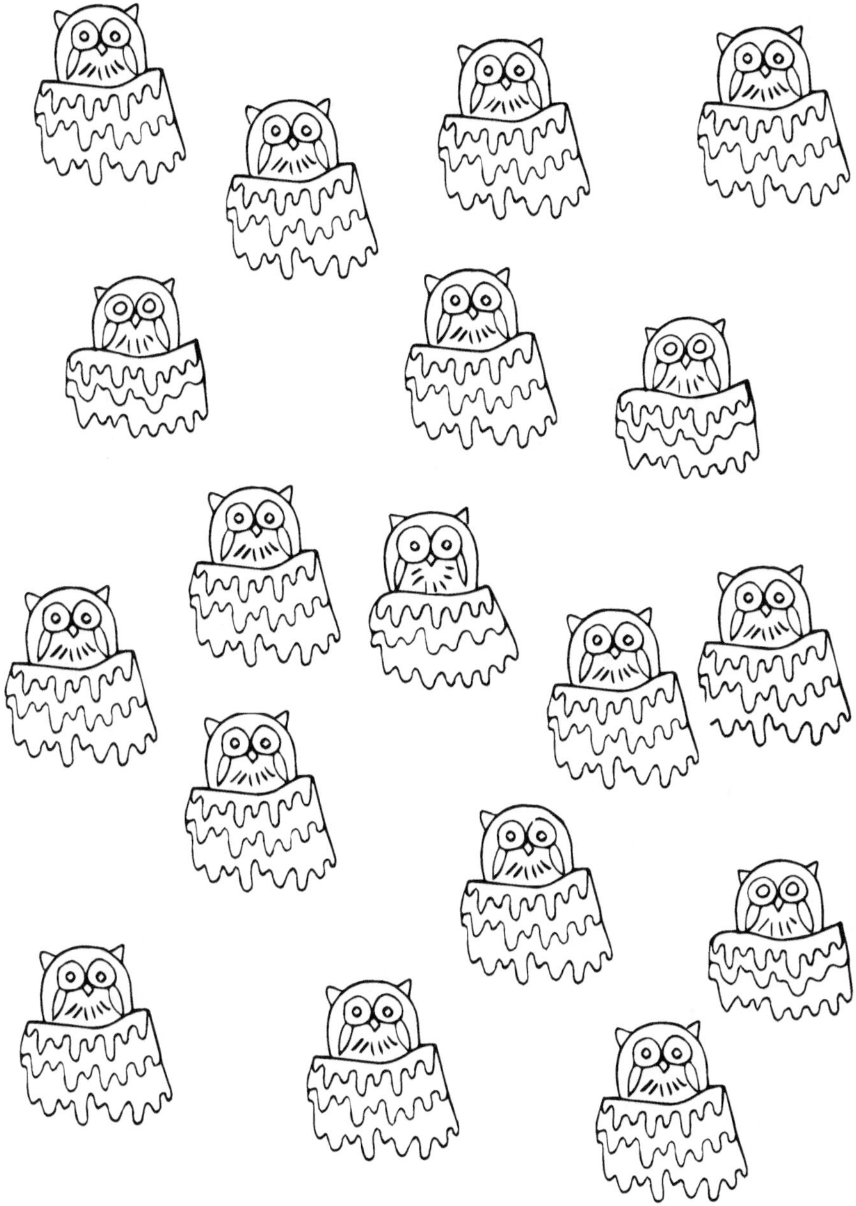

www.ingramcontent.com/pod-product-compliance
Lightning Source LLC
Chambersburg PA
CBHW072139170526
45158CB00004BA/1429
9780997166002